LESBIAN PHILOSOPHY:
EXPLORATIONS

JEFFNER ALLEN

LESBIAN PHILOSOPHY:

EXPLORATIONS

INSTITUTE OF LESBIAN STUDIES
Palo Alto, California

Grateful acknowledgment for permission to print material from earlier versions of my essays is extended to Acacia Press, ''Remembering: A Time I Will Be My Own Beginning''; Roman & Allanheld, ''Motherhood: The Annihilation of Women''; *TRIVIA: A Journal of Ideas,* ''Looking at Our Blood: A Lesbian Response to Men's Terrorization of Women.''

FIRST EDITION

Cover design: Nicole Morisset
Photograph: Lynda Koolish
Typography: Ann Flanagan

Library of Congress Cataloging-in-Publication Data

Allen, Jeffner, 1947–
  Lesbian philosophy.

  1. Lesbianism.   I. Title.
HQ75.5.A45   1986   306.7'663   85-24016
ISBN 0-934903-86-7

1   2   3   4   5   6   7   8   9

That our love of lesbian language and experience may bring us further in our discovery of freedom.

CONTENTS

Preface   9

Remembering:
    A Time I Will Be My Own Beginning   13

Looking at Our Blood:
    A Lesbian Response to Men's Terrorization
    of Women   27

Motherhood:
    The Annihilation of Women   61

The Naming of Difference:
    Truth and Female Friendship   89

Notes   109

PREFACE

Lesbian Philosophy evokes the intensity of lesbian passions, which jolt the patriarchal order. My desire to know the worlds of my experience breaks with their more than two thousand year absence in Western philosophy. In the sensuous ambience of a new exuberance, I find my lively subjectivity, which when cultivated with tenderness, moves toward *a knowledge so vivid it can be touched.*

I have written this book by drawing concepts from experience. Some of these sketches have emerged at that moment of discovery just at the edge of language and experience. Surprising concepts often have arrived with laughter, or have been brought to me by others, along with conversation, hugs, and a kiss. Concepts dug into painful, torturous moments I have transformed into life preserving weapons.

The fiercely Amazon sentiment of these explorations is close to my heart. I choose to exercise a lesbian violence that uproots the dictates of heterosexual virtue. I am not wo-man, the counterpart of men. I will not be the maker of objects and ideas that are in the service of men. I gather myself in a time, space, and history that are shaped by the events of my life.

Solitary and with friends, I have written *Lesbian Philosophy* sensing the urgency of a present time in which it is

9

possible to live, freely. I would like to thank Sarah Hoagland, Marjorie Larney, Paula Moseley, Julia Penelope, Joyce Trebilcot, and Lise Weil for their thoughtful comments. To the extent that I have realized such a present, I thank, especially, Julie Murphy.

REMEMBERING:

A TIME I WILL BE
MY OWN BEGINNING

Touching, feeling, imagining, fighting, thinking, caressing, I remember myself. I remember the possibilities in my future, the actuality of my past, the openness of my present. I remember the members of my body, the actions that form my body as lived. In remembering, I am.

Remembering shapes my existence within a temporal horizon. The horizon of temporality is not neutral. Whenever the profiles of my memory, like the horizons of time, are erected by men, I cannot remember myself. At such moments, male domination not infrequently forces me to remember myself as essentially and "by nature" the Other who "is" only in relation to men. I, dismembered, disappear into nonexistence.

Yet, quite clearly, I am here. In everyday life I undergo and envision an experience of stopping the time and memories of patriarchy and of unfolding a temporality in which I am myself.

According to mythic history, in late Mycenaean times the oracle engaged in a remembering of herself. As a priestess of the earth goddess, Ge, she descended into Earth's caverns and returned with prophetic wisdom. Whenever the oracle spoke of a community's past, future, or present, she remembered ahead of, back into, and within herself as a source.[1]

The Delphic oracle remembered herself as an originary source of time-consciousness and historical being—until Apollo killed her. The Delphic oracle, embodied as a female dragon, was slain by Apollo. Apollo appropriated and occupied the oracle's prophetic tripod. Zeus stopped Earth from sending dreams to warn humans of the oracle's impending danger. Chronos, with the passing of time, turned the dragon into a male so it would be a more "worthy" opponent for Apollo to combat.

I remember, only with great difficulty, the oracle who was an originary source of time and history. When I look back at the so-called "origins" of Western civilization, I see the Pythia who is *not* herself. The Delphic oracle is said to remember because Apollo possesses her: "At Delphi ...Apollo relied on 'enthusiasm' in its original and literal sense. The Pythia became *entheos, plena, deo:* the god entered into her and used her vocal chords as if they were his own."[2] Apollo becomes he who shapes the horizons of time and history. He commands wars and peace, decrees laws, legislates art and music.

The oracle, robbed of her memories and bodily members, becomes the vehicle of Apollo's utterances. She is made to sit on Apollo's ritual tripod and, finally, is replaced by a male priest called "the Prophet."

Today it is neither possible nor, perhaps, even desirable to return to the originary remembering of the Delphic oracle of mythic history. What is significant is the oracle's meaning, and loss of meaning, for me as I remember myself.

I. Dismemberment

From the Delphic oracle to modern times, men's expulsion of Mnemosyne, she who remembers, has attempted to make impossible the free, open and spontaneous, remembering of ourselves. Whenever our history has passed through the events of ancient European culture, we have been forced into dismemberment.

As we reproduce, are forced to reproduce, the world shaped by men, the demise of the oracle at Delphi continues. *Reproductive remembering: men's attempt to impregnate women by force.* Just as God, man's absolute and reified idea of himself, once placed thoughts of the True, the Good, and the Beautiful in men, man attempts to implant his ideas in women. Women, subjected to forced insemination, become filled, saturated with the man-become-god. Surrounded by the dominating power of man-become-god, we are made pregnable [from *prendre,* to take], understood in its literal sense as vulnerable to capture, taken. Time after time, we are forced to have "his" child, to reproduce "his" words, thoughts, actions. Like the Delphic oracle who must announce not herself, but the time and history of man, "his" teleology, we are obliged to name not ourselves, but the life of the species, man and "his" immortality. The result is our forced sterilization. Women cannot be genuinely pregnant [*preg-nas,* akin to *gignere,* to reproduce]. We cannot produce ourselves. The horizons of our time and history are bare. Sterilized against our will, we are fragmented, dismembered.

We are dismembered as men impress, cut, carve into us the styles and memories of our embodiment. Our memories must be "representational," must repeat and re-present the time and history of patriarchy. Our memories must relive without question the patriarchal world, as if we were "fitting a foot in its own footmark to reflect recognition."[3] Whatever we remember must correspond to, fit into, the mark which men, the measure of all things, have drawn in advance to limit and define our existence. The shape of the footmark, and of the foot which is supposed to make the mark, is determined by the marker, by he who binds women's feet until they fit the shape he has prescribed. Whenever the print left by our feet is deemed "incorrect," that is, does not represent the world imprinted on us by men, we are judged "unfit."

Man, like Apollo, assumes an unlimited power for calculating, planning, and molding all things to fit the authority of "his" time and history. Men thereby place women at a distance from our own experience, and from the world made by men. Men make women the Other. Our position as the Other, who "is" only in relation to men, becomes normative and binding. Our memory, possessed, as it were, by men, is confined to the reproduction of our dismemberment.

Our responses to our dismemberment through reproductive memory and representational thought are varied:

My experiences and memories are violated. I become like a *blank tablet,* "a good thick slab of wax, smooth and kneaded to the right consistency." I am rendered "blank," without a time and history of my own. The images of patriarchy are "stamped" on the "tablets of my heart." I am compelled to forget myself, for the imprints of patriarchy are "clear and deep enough to last a long time."[4]

At other times, my memory becomes an *aviary* "stocked with birds of every sort, some in flocks apart from the rest, some in small groups, and some solitary, flying in any direction among them all."[5] Yet, however brightly the birds, or images of my memory, may sing, they are caged. My memories, bound by the patriarchal frame of reproductive memory, are not free. A flock of birds, a string of images, instantly triggers a chain of memories...a series of habits impressed into my body...habits pre-formed by men to ensure my adaptation to not being myself: to not being. Re-active to the most compelling images of my reproductive memory, I repeat the elements of patriarchy. I remain a blank slate.

In still another instance, my memory may be that of a *gatekeeper.* Like the Delphic oracle who is made to sit on the tripod of Apollo, I may take on, be forced to take on, patriarchy's imprinting of my memory. I may even attempt to keep other women in line with such imprints. When designated by men as the keeper of patriarchal obedience, I may assume the task of impressing on women a conduct deemed "fitting" and "correct."

Reproductive memory pulls women who imprint women ...all of whom are imprinted by men, into collective dismemberment. Still safeguarding the most brightly plumed of deceptive images, we begin to adjust, albeit uncomfortably, to the power of men. We try to keep afloat by assuming a man-made memory whose horizon is the static reproductive impression, forever confined to and measured by what "is." Limited, unable to think myself other than as I appear to men, I approach paralysis. The static mode of my temporal horizon confirms the static aspect of my existence. Without the free and open becoming of time, I die.

Nevertheless, to survive [*super-vivere*] is to live on, to continue to exist after a death. In my memory there is, always and already, a crack between those images with which I am inseminated and those which I live, a split between what I am told I "ought" to remember and what I actually experience. My memory, as a "gatekeeper" for men, neutralizes this rupture. Although knowing that my foot does not fit the footprint made for it, I try to walk as if it did.

Yet, while living daily a static existence, holding on for dear life (and for certain death), I may ask: On to what am

I holding? And why? With the demise of myself as a static object, reproductive remembering reaches its limit.

II. The Between

When I recollect, my memory folds over upon itself. The oracle has been expelled not once, but over and over again. Yet, something of her remains.

Amidst an unending series of images possessed by men, a moment quite different in kind appears. Surrounded by its possibility, I may, perhaps, exclaim, "I hate men!" After all, as Adrienne Rich writes:

> Am I to go on saying
> for myself, for her
>
> *This is my body*
> Take and destroy it?[6]

Between the static present of reproductive memory and the possibility of remembering otherwise, man-hating emerges as having been just below the surface.

A cautionary voice of the gatekeeper's memory may promptly echo the command of patriarchy: One ought not hate men. Joanna Russ states in "The New Misandry":

> It's nothing new for the oppressed to be solemnly told that their entry to Heaven depends on not hating their oppressors....[1] You do something nasty to me. [2] I hate you. [3] You find it uncomfortable to be hated. [4] You think how nice it would be if I didn't hate you. [5] You decide I ought not to hate you because hate is bad. [6] Good people don't hate. [7] Because I hate I am a bad person. [8] It is not what you did to me that makes me hate you, it is my own bad nature. *I—not you—am the cause of my hating you.*[7]

I may echo the voices of men, "Be assertive, not aggressive. Don't confront: don't hate men." Perhaps I need "positive thinking," a "personality change." Am I OK? Am I "hung up"? Smile! Smile! It's not "normal." Don't hate men. Hate myself—that's fitting for women. Selective amnesia begins again.

But NO. Man-hating is not a matter of taste. It depends not upon my personal whim. Man-hating is my response to men's violence against women. According to FBI statistics alone, every three minutes a woman is raped and every eighteen seconds a woman is beaten—by a man.[8] *The ultimate mark of man's possession of women may well be the ethic of suppression by which he forbids women to hate him.*

A faint voice of the gatekeeper's memory may propose, with the greatest of diplomacy, "I hate not men but what it is men do in this culture."[9] To hate the "sin" but love the "sinner" continues, however, a patriarchal and Christian morality that posits a pure human nature, or essence, behind men's actions. According to Thomas Aquinas, hatred is always preceded by and arises from love. Hatred is a disorder of the will and the root of sin. One cannot hate God in his essence, for God's essence is Goodness. Likewise, one cannot hate one's neighbor, for hatred would be opposed to the love that we have "naturally" for him.[10] I deny all essential characteristics men have assigned to women and claim that we are our actions. With regard to men, however, I, the diplomat, am caught in dangerous patriarchal essentialism: I insist that men are essentially good, regardless of their actions.

If I say, "I hate not men but what they do," I remain divided against myself, dismembered. I hate myself and not my oppressor. In contrast, when I say, "I hate men," I use language well. I say what I experience. *I hate men*

▽   ▽   ▽

Man-hating may be considered an antagonistic division between object (woman) and subject (man). Woman, the supposedly passive object who can be only in relation to men, rebels against and ruptures with man, the transcendent subject and Creator.

Man-hating is not, however, the "battle of the sexes." It is not an incessant cycle of men vs. women, women vs. men. Nor is man-hating a "heroic hatred." Heroic hatred is insatiable; upon vanquishing its enemy, heroic hatred goes off to seek another. Man-hating places in question all heroic ability, all antagonistic activity that exists solely for its own sake. Man-hating threatens at its core the patriarchal world of strife and fragmentation.

Man-hating posits an end to the conditions that set it in motion. Man-hating is without the ineffectiveness of resentment. Anger alone no longer suffices, for in anger I must act against an individual who has power over me, rising to his level to get even. My anger, instead, turns to, and is grounded in, hatred. Hatred begins with the assumption that there is an equality between woman and man and ends in the breakdown of all patriarchal definitions of women.

My hatred of myself appears in a new perspective. Hatred of wo-man is hatred of that aspect of myself that is bound to man, of myself as the twin essence, or "wife" of man.

▽　　▽　　▽

I break with reproductive memory. I no longer claim to be wo-man, the counterpart of man, she who is possessed by men. *I posit my own freedom. I place myself with all who will be women no longer: lesbians.*

Man-hating brings me memories of strength by which I gather myself in productive remembering. Man-hating is, in its most profound sense, grief at an injustice, a deep bereavement and caring.[11]

Guided by etymology, the echo of my deep though often hidden experience, I find that "to hate" is to experience an absence of justice, a violation of one's rights, a state of being injured, oppressed. Hatred is grievance at an injustice. Hatred includes the pain and sorrow, fear and anger, originating from an injury. Hatred is a deep and poignant distress caused by bereavement. Just as anger is grounded in hatred, hatred is lodged in grief. Hatred emerges in grief for the dead, funeral rites, mourning. My hatred arises from a loss, but not the loss of my "other half," as patriarchal dualists engaged in preserving forever the twin essences man and woman, or masculine and feminine, often say. My hatred of men is, rather, my experience of the loss of myself and others as autonomous subjects. My man-hating is grief for myself and other women at the loss of our bodies and memories, time and history.

At the same time, to hate [from Old English *hete,* akin to Old High German *haz,* hate, and Greek *kēdos,* care] is also to care: for a deceased friend, for a living friend, intimate and beloved, for a group of persons or communities. The opposite of hate is "not caring" [*akēdia*], apathy, sloth. My intense and active love for what is most intimate, most dear, may be accompanied by man-hating. If I say, "I hate men," it is because men continue to bereave women of ourselves as free autonomous subjects *and* because I continue to care for myself and those intimates close to me as individuals who are whole and free.

Integral to remembering is man-hating: a difficult stance because it requires a fidelity to what is real in ourselves.[12] My memory, folded over upon itself, remembers itself. Once violated by man, it breaks with his violence.

III. Mnemosyne

Mnemosyne, she who remembers, is mindful of, and full of care for, the body of my experience.[13] I draw together my experience, with its ever-changing horizon of future, past, and present. I discover my body anew in its connectedness. *In productive remembering, my memory remembers itself.*

Productive memory is concerned neither with "correctness," fitting in with the static fragmentation of patriarchal actuality, nor with "repetition," representing a specific historical period from the patriarchal past. Remembering, in its most primoridal sense, constitutes a time and history in which I will be my own beginning. Remembering moves . . . always on the way in another way, in another direction.

Remembering that reminds brings to mind and keeps in mind often painful events, critically analyzing them for the purpose of change. I articulate in anticipatory retrospection, "a history which looks backward in order to move forward: a history not just to give credit but to record, to record attempts and mistakes, not just accomplishments, a history to use, an 'arsenal' for women."[14] Aware of the dangers of falling into an illusory future, a false past, and a spurious present, I establish an honest and incisive history of even the most dreadful events.

Remembering that gathers focuses on the often silent history of women's culture: the daily connections between women, women as lovers, workers, friends. With care for what has fallen into oblivion, I make present the similarities and differences of women's experiences. I recover my life with other women.

Remembering that frees moves toward the dissolution of the class wo-man, the "females of men,"[15] into a free and spontaneous subjectivity. I place radically in question that which I have remembered, granting my memory an ongoing self-reflexivity and openness:

> Elsa Brauer says...There was a time when you were not a class, remember that....You say you have lost all recollection of it, remember....You say there are no words to describe this time, you say it does not exist. But remember. Make an effort to remember. Or, failing that, invent.[16]

Remembering forward into the open, as yet unknown, I claim the temporal horizon of the possible, where everything must begin again.

Springing forth from caverns deep in the earth, Mnemosyne designates a central aspect of my self-constitution.

The persistence of my dismemberment is but an indication of the fragments and limbs of women which appear in the field of patriarchy. With care, found at the center of my hatred for men, I remember those fragments into a time when women are with women, a time, even, when wo-men as a class can disappear. The caverns of Mnemosyne speak anew only when I hear, as it were, "the echo / of an echo in a shell," when unaccustomed memories and a new attunement to remembering bring me "through spiral upon spiral of a shell / of memory that yet connects us." [17]

LOOKING AT OUR BLOOD:

A LESBIAN RESPONSE TO MEN'S TERRORIZATION OF WOMEN

I am my blood, my life, my body. Terrorized, I am blood-less, without life, without body.

To recognize terror as a reality in my life is to acknowledge the real possibility of my fragmentation, death, bloodlessness. To see terror and to see through terror to myself is to claim my life apart from, in rupture with, the constructs of male domination. The male-established boundaries of state and transnational corporate structures are not those which I, a woman, must defend first if I am to exist at all; the boundaries I must defend first are those of my body, my life blood, my world.

I. Terror

Terror is men's power to instill fear in all women through the threat and accomplishment of female fragmentation and death. Men's terrorization of women is indiscriminate: it can be done by any man to any woman at any time. Within the world of men's creation, men's terrorization of women is inevitable. Every moment women are forced to function for men in a situation where our freedom, choice, and genuine alternatives have no meaning, our fear, horror, and sheer terror increase. In men's reign of terror the general community of women lives in dread of outrage and possible death.

Ordinarily this situation would be called a war, for what is dear is threatened with destruction. Yet, men's terrorization of women appears not as a war, but as a matter of course. Under men's rule of terror, my blood becomes invisible.

The weapon of terror and the specific war crime against women is realized centrally, and most completely, in rape. Rapists are the "shock troops" of male supremacy.[1] For both rapist and court judge, coercive sexuality may be the norm: "This is more like an attempted seduction than it is sexual assault, albeit a little rough, but this is the way I remember it."[2] The fact that men who murder women are, in almost three out of four instances, the women's husbands and lovers[3] further reinforces rape as "the primary heterosexual mode for relating."[4] Like all terror tactics, rape is indiscriminate but not arbitrary: rape is punishment for being a woman.

The objective structure of male politics declares that all women need a penis, all women need a man. Within the ideology of male entitlement, a woman exists to be "empenised." She is legitimately subject to taking a penis, taking a man, at any time and in any circumstances selected for her by male power. Men's terrorization of women attempts to guarantee that no woman, neither she who "chooses" men in specific situations nor she who does not "choose" men in any situation, can leave, or change, the objective structure under which all women live. Woman, the male social construct, is terrorized to always need a penis, to always need a man.

II. The Negation of Terror

Terror is made visible in the unfreedom of my body: "Terror is the now when he puts an insistent hand on my waist."[5] Terror is negated through the freedom of my body, my thinking and acting in the living presence of our blood. As I create and exercise my freedom, as I befriend and love what is gentle and dear, I negate terror.

Nonviolence as a Patriarchal Construct

Patriarchal formulation of the theme of nonviolence vs. violence has functioned, since the earliest of times, as a fundamental obstacle to, and primary mode of disregard for, women's freedom. Helen Diner writes of the significance of the defeat of the Amazons, the Thermodotines, by the Greeks:

> At the celebrations in honor of the dead, Demosthenes, Lysias, Himerios, Ioscrates, and Arsteides praise the victory over the Amazons as more important than that over the Persians or any other deed in history...
> The wars between Greeks and Persians were wars

between two male-dominated societies. In the Amazon war, the issue was which of the two forms of life was to shape European civilization in its image.[6]

In the Amazon form of life, women are self-governing, founding cities and carrying on agriculture in strength and harmony. In the Greek form of life, violence and nonviolence are defined by the language and actions of men. Violence is assigned to men, nonviolence to women. Men's domination of women, often to the point of women's ultimate death, is thereby legitimized and perpetuated.

In celebration of our dead we honor three Amazon queens of Phrygia, Hippolyte, Antiope, and Oreithyia, all of whom became objects of the male-defined violence inherent in the classical Greek way of life. Hippolyte is slain when Theseus and his warriors invade Phrygia. Antiope is carried off by Theseus and forced into marriage. Oreithyia, upon finding Hippolyte dead and Antiope abducted, departs for Greece with her Amazon army. Though weakened by the voyage, Oreithyia and her army invade Athens and occupy the Acropolis for four months. Antiope, living the deathly lie of co-optation, fights at the side of her husband and son—against the Amazons—until killed by one of her own. Forced to a compromise and in retreat, Oreithyia dies of grief.

In the war of the Greeks against the Amazons, the daily life and freedom of the Amazons is violated. Women, from that moment on, are defined as nonviolent and as existing necessarily in relation to men and male violence. Amazons

who refuse to accept the Greek view of women as beings-
to-be-empenised are killed because they refuse to be nonviolent. Antiope, the Amazon who temporarily accepts
and conforms to the Greek notion of women and its corol-
lary, that all women must be Mothers,[7] beings who produce
for the sake of men, experiences a living death as the nonviolent ally of male violence. From the defeat of the Amazons, and continuing in varied forms throughout history,
women, whether Amazons or Mothers, are constrained to
exist within the structures of male violence, and to exist
there nonviolently, that is, as beings who are dead or who
are on their way to certain death.

Nonviolence as a women's issue is reaffirmed decisively
for the modern period by patriarchy's recovery of the suffragist movement at the turn of the century. Against and
apart from the structures of male hegemony, which attempt
to define women as peacemakers throughout history, stand
the words and deeds of militant suffragists in the nineteenth
century. In 1898 Laura Clay poses the issue of militant
suffragism in her article, "Can Women Be Fighters?" Clay
writes, "It is by no means self-evident that women are
naturally unfitted for fighting or are unwarlike in disposition," and makes reference to "the traditions of Amazons"
in support of her thesis.[8]

Similarly, the Women's Social and Political Union,
WSPU, led by Emmeline Pankhurst and her daughters
Sylvia and Christabel, takes on the motto, "Deeds, not

Words." In response to the horror and atrocity imposed on the British suffragists, the WSPU intensifies its militancy: October, 1910, the WSPU declares war against men's violence; March, 1911, Emmeline Pankhurst states, "We have made more progress by breaking glass than when we allowed them to break our heads"; January, 1912, at Parliament's defeat of the conciliation bill, Emmeline Pankhurst declares, "I will incite this meeting to rebellion." When the New Suffrage Bill is ruled out of order in the House of Commons, January, 1912, the WSPU effectively isolates London from the rest of the country. Telegraph wires are cut, postal service stopped, museums, art galleries, golf courses, exclusive clubs and public parks are invaded and closed down. The women march, six thousand strong, in a funeral procession for the suffragist Emily Davidson.[9] Because Emmeline Pankhurst and the WSPU see women's bodies broken by men, and as never to be broken again by men, they choose to act outside the male-legislated definition of women as nonviolent.

Militant suffragists look at their own bodies, life, blood. They act passionately to create and exercise their freedom. Elizabeth Robins, author of "Woman's War: A Defense of Militant Suffrage," 1912, writes of police brutality toward the suffragists and asks,

> Is it rational to expect these experiences to leave a woman unchanged? If she were to remain unchanged, would she not prove herself more insensate than the brutes? People who would insist that such things shall

leave a woman unmoved are not merely those who would deny her right to ballot: they would deny her right to the feelings of a human being.[10]

Robins affirms, in her response, not the perpetuation of women as nonviolent, but women's self-governance in all spheres.

The strength of action by militant suffragists such as Laura Clay, Emmeline Pankhurst, and Elizabeth Robins is quickly challenged by men, as well as by those women who view themselves in the tradition of peacemakers and Mothers. At the end of the nineteenth century, Oreithyia is still undermined by Antiope. In the United States, 1887, Susan B. Anthony writes of the modern-day Antiope, whose loyalties lie with husband and son, rather than with herself as a free woman,

> Your suggestion [regarding women's right to vote] means a revolution which women will not create against their own fathers, husbands, brothers and sons. A whole race of men under a foreign or tyrannical government, like the Cubans, may rise in rebellion, but for women thus to band themselves against the power enthroned in their own households is quite another matter.[11]

Unlike the times of antiquity, by the turn of the century there are far more women who view themselves as Mothers than as Amazons, and more Mothers than Amazons who engage in the political sphere. The English National Union

33

of Women's Suffrage Societies, for instance, works for reform exclusively through peaceful and parliamentary means. Labeled sympathetically by men of their time as "sane, sensible, and never discouraged," they disavow, publically and repeatedly, the militant endeavors of the WSPU.[12] So successful is the society of Fathers, Sons, and Mothers, that by 1914 the WSPU is never heard from again. British women turn to war work and, in 1917, women demonstrate as war workers, not as suffragists, although it is still eleven years before complete women's suffrage is granted.

In the United States, likewise, militant women's rights leaders who acknowledge the war only by such slogans as "Freedom Begins at Home" are terrorized.[13] The society of Mothers, caring more about the good of a country ruled by men than about its own well-being, proves its patriotism by turning its energy to support of the United States' entry into World War I. On both continents, women as Mothers nonviolently support patriotism, both in collaboration with male society in the de-radicalization of the women's rights movement and in coalition with patriarchy in the war movement.

At the beginning of the twentieth century, women as Mothers remain nonviolent, by male standards, thereby reinforcing the male supremacist framework in which women are to think and act in relation to men, as objects subordinate to the violence of men. Women as Mothers defend the boundaries of men's territories, but not the boundaries of women's bodies. Men's renewed success in abducting women from genuine women's concerns, conjoined with

34

women's increasing self-identification as nonviolent, leads to patriarchy's recovery of the women's liberation movement. The bond that men proclaim between women and nonviolence becomes the condition for men's successful terrorization of women and for development of an ideology of nonviolence that has nothing to do with women's creation of genuine freedom. As women, it becomes increasingly difficult for us to look at our blood, that is, to see the reality and possibility of Amazonian harmony and strength.

Heterosexual Virtue

The ideology of heterosexual virtue forms the cornerstone of the designation of women as nonviolent. The ideology of heterosexual virtue charges women to be "moral," virtuously nonviolent in the face of the "political," the violent male-defined world. The ideology of heterosexual virtue entitles men to terrorize—possess, humiliate, violate, objectify—women and forecloses the possibility of women's active response to men's sexual terrorization. Women, constrained to nonviolence, are precluded from claiming and creating a self, a world. The moral imperative established by heterosexual virtue, that women are to be nonviolent, establishes a male-defined good that is beneficial to men and harmful to women.

Prescriptive claims concerning *what a woman is* are linked frequently to discussion of the virtue of nonviolence.

Heterosexual virtue posits women, nonviolent beings having the power to give life, in juxtaposition to men, violent beings having the power to risk life and to take life. Whereas woman, the moral voice, gives birth, man, the political creature, gives death. The reasons why women have such "uniquely female abilities and knowledge"[14] are usually located either in socio-biology or socio-morality. According to the former, society is formed by purported biological differences in hormones, "aggression levels," "sex drives," etc. For the latter, society is shaped by a moralizing, usually quasi-religious belief concerning male and female "character traits."

Adherents to the ideology of heterosexual virtue hold in common the claim that violence is brutalizing. Women are held to be better than men, either wholly or in part, precisely because women are nonviolent. Women's superiority is frequently attributed to feminine qualities of nurturance, understanding, and concern for others. The history of nurturance, in which women give freely, expect nothing in return, and remain powerless while partaking in unsatisfying relationships, is dismissed. Obliterated, as well, are women who have rejected feminine qualities as false virtues that are restrictive and useless for women's daily lives.

An appeal to a special relationship between mother and child, emerging in acts of childbirth, nursing, and caretaking of the young, often is made to justify the claim of women's superiority. Disregarded in full is the ineffectiveness of motherly virtue and nonviolence. Ignored are the implications of situations such as the Irish Women's Peace

Movement where, precisely because no attempt is made by the movement leaders to involve women "in any other terms than as mothers of families," the women routinely and futilely "take themselves into the street, say prayers, sing hymns and go home again."[15]

If women are to avoid becoming like men, women must reject the use of violence—this is the practical consequence of the ideology of heterosexual virtue. With respect to women's present existence, Ynestra King, of the Women's Pentagon Action, states, "the reason women are different is because we do different things, and if we do things like kill men, we will become like them."[16] With regard to women's future, Pamela McAllister asks that we "...refrain from using power we haven't had (i.e., muscles, guns, etc.)."[17] What it is to be a woman, that is, nonviolent and therefore different from men, is thereby preserved at the greatest cost—the risk of women's freedom.

The heterosexual virtue which binds women to male-defined nonviolence is preeminently self-destructive, leading to the sole form of action permitted to women: martyrdom and suicide. To accept the patriarchal construct of nonviolence vs. violence is to side with men's terrorization of women and against women, its avoiders, resisters, and fervent opponents. By assigning to women the project of nonviolence, heterosexual virtue focuses the cause of women's victimization on women, blames the victim, tries to reform the victim, but never challenges the ideology of male entitlement which itself creates woman as a construct.

The heterosexual virtue that dictates what is a woman also prescribes *what is violence*. Violence is defended as the right to limit life and take life that is exercised by men, for men and against women. A woman, by definition, is not violent, and if violent, a female is not a woman.

Women, in keeping with the constraints of heterosexual virtue, give priority with increasing frequency to the avoidance of exercising violence, rather than to the creation of freedom. That the only definition of violence and nonviolence is that legislated by heterosexual virtue is presupposed without question, for instance, by Peggy Kornegger's "Cosmic Anarchism: Lesbians in the Sky with Diamonds." The article reaffirms Barbara Deming's claim that violence is "the intent to kill or physically violate (as in rape)," and nonviolence is "antiviolent resistance," that is, "learning self-defense, learning to fight back, but *without* intent to kill, admittedly someone could get killed anyway...but the chances of death would be *less*...if the intent is *not* to kill."[18] The emphasis is on not killing, rather than on staying free.

The much-cited exhortation from Emma Goldman, that "the means used be identical in spirit and tendency with the purpose to be achieved," is employed in a similarly unliberating manner. In reference to the means-end argument, Barbara Deming says, "if one wants a nonviolent society, one must act in a way to achieve that not only without violence but against violence."[19] Yet, such a position remains within the structures of heterosexual virtue, which presupposes one world and one set of linguistic and existential definitions.

Implicit in heterosexual virtue is faith in a magical teleology that will tilt the balance scale so that violence, as male-defined, will be replaced some time in the future by nonviolence, as male-defined. However, a teleology immanent to patriarchy, in which one male construct is miraculously substituted for another, does not get women anywhere but where we are already—oppressed.

The teleology of heterosexual virtue presupposes an understanding of peace as a precarious balance trick, a compromise, in which one mode of unfreedom is exchanged for another.[20] Such an appeal to peace as a patchwork in which one set of elements, nonviolence, predominates over another, violence, ignores the possibility of living openly in a state of genuine harmony and well-being. The exuberance and harmony of the Amazons is erased by women as Mothers who, as in the *Lysistrata,* settle for keeping all pieces of the world together, even though no part of that world enhances women's freedom.

The prescriptions of heterosexual virtue enforce the powerlessness of women. After all, whose chances for escape could possibly be worse if women, even when life-endangered, must give first priority to not killing, rather than to keeping free? To continue to place nonviolence above freedom suggests that my aversion to violence must be stronger than my aversion to my own death. As Ti-Grace Atkinson already pointed out, early in the "second wave" of the women's liberation movement, "violence for her

39

friends, we all accept. Our enemies we worry about."[21] The practical effect of heterosexual virtue is to reinforce women's position in the hell of men's deadly inferno.

Heterosexual virtue *demands that women endure violence from men of all colors—in silence.* On the basis of race, be it the racial identity or the racial difference between a woman and her assailant, women are pressured not to speak about, or to report, sexual violence. Claims about black, yellow, brown, white, red skin colors are used by hetero-sexual virtue as reasons to justify or to excuse rape. Male enforcers of and female adherents to heterosexual virtue may even affirm rape as an act of rebellion, that is, rebellion against men and male society, rather than as an act of oppression, namely, oppression against women.

Yet, a woman is never raped by blackness or whiteness. It is men, and manly actions, that rape women. Men, as sexual terrorists, utilize rape as a weapon of revenge against men, as an infringement on other men's "property." A rapist may even engage in a verbal dialogue with another man whose presence he imagines during the rape. The rapist, a white man, declares himself more powerful than the black man to whom the black woman he is raping is assumed to belong: the rapist, a man of color, claims to be more pow-erful than the white man to whom the white woman he is raping is assumed to belong. The man who raped me says, "Look at it, have you ever seen such a big dick before? Have you ever made love to a black man before? I bet you haven't. Bet you've never seen such a big one before. I'm big. Suppose we had met somewhere else, in a little restaurant around the corner. You're such a nice girl. Would you have liked me? I bet you've never made love like this before. I'm big. Does your man fuck you good? When your man comes home you better be still about this or I'll blow your head off." It is a white man to whom one rapist, a black man, compares himself, in relation to whom he claims to have more power.

Conversely, as the police drive with me through the neighborhood later, purporting to look for the rapist, they imagine and name the missing man an "animal." It is a black man to whom those particular white policemen compare themselves, in relation to whom they claim to have more power.

In both conversations, *all* of the men's talk about another man, whose presence they imagine, is, in effect, a monologue by men about an invisible woman. It is the woman whose presence is never acknowledged. Men, both white and black, assert their identity as oppressors in that both gain in stature, both earn blood money, by ignoring my subjectivity and viewing me as a being to be "empenised."

The heterosexual virtue that enhances the bonds between men who rape weakens the possible community between women who are the victims and survivors of rape. Heterosexual virtue uses differences between women to encourage women's loyalties to all men, or to men of certain skin colors, above women's identification with any woman.

41

Women who identify with the social and power status of men who are white in such a way as to speak only of men of color as rapists, and women who claim as their own the social and power standing of men of color in such a manner as to mention only white men as rapists, continue men's terrorism of all women. Such identification perpetuates sexism and racism, for it implies that the men whose acts of rape are not mentioned, on the basis of color alone, either need not, or cannot, act in ways that are fully human, i.e., that are not oppressive to over half the human race—women.

The society of Mothers accepts patriarchy's account of the primary reason for its fall from supposed bliss—women. When we, as Amazons, defend ourselves and act for ourselves, Fathers, Sons, and Mothers hold us responsible for society's reprisals against us. Women's liberation is termed the cause of the alleged increase in violence against women. Women who do not remain nonviolent, as dictated by men, are called responsible for men's fear of women. What is seldom asked is why any man should be afraid of a woman's freedom—unless he wants to terrorize her, unless he is already on the side of the rapist.

A Lesbian Violence

Why the ideology of heterosexual virtue continues to succeed in abducting women from genuine women's concerns might be attributed to women mistaking enforced passivity for authentic subjectivity, or giving birth to patriarchy for giving birth to ourselves. The predominance of the heterosexual virtue of women as nonviolent may also rest on the difficulty of seeing outside its hegemony to an actionary world of lesbian strength, power, and harmony. There, as Monique Wittig states, "it is necessary to do away with this myth of fragile, decorative, feminine homosexuality, without danger for heterosexuality, that is, recoverable by it."[22]

The freedom of a lesbian world originates from a specific form of violent activity: the passionate energy to tear apart and put together anew almost everything we believe and live, to create a new and freeing subjectivity. Unlike the patriarchal breaking and fragmentation of woman's body, legitimated by the heterosexual prescription that posits the difference of nonviolence to distinguish women from men, "here the body is constantly pieced back together again, lovingly...woman's wholeness, rather than her difference, inscribes itself on the text, on the language, and into the culture."[23] The world of lesbian strength, power, and harmony emerges which is neither the inversion of

43

patriarchy, that is, nonviolent by male definition, nor the same as the world of men, that is, violent by male definition.

The society of Amazons, like WITCH, Women's International Terrorist Conspiracy from Hell, remembers that women were "the first guerilla and resistance fighters against oppression—the oppression of women."[24] As Mary Daly suggests, male hegemony authorizes one, but not the only, conception of violence: "The malevolence of male violence (which is, in fact, usually dispassionate) is misnamed *anger,* masking the fact that women are The Enemy against whom all patriarchal wars are waged, and muting righteous female anger."[25] Lesbian anger responds to patriarchal prescription by recognizing that men's violence is the institutionalized violence of patriarchy and, as such, cannot legitimize other forms of violence that are directed against itself.[26]

Whereas men's prescriptions concerning violence constrain me to unfreedom, *as lesbian, I define and exercise the violence necessary to achieve my freedom.* I acknowledge de Beauvoir's statement:

> Violence is the authentic proof of each one's loyalty to himself, to his will; radically to deny this will is to deny oneself any objective truth, it is to wall oneself up in an abstract subjectivity; anger or revolt that does not get into the muscles remains a figment of the imagination. It is a profound frustration not to be able to register one's feelings upon the face of the world.[27]

I would differentiate, however, as de Beauvoir does not, between the male-defined violence of patriarchy, which assumes the constant conjunction of violence and non-violence, active and passive, powerful and powerless—and a liberating violence that is lesbian. As the Editorial Collective of *Questions Féministes* writes,

> We must reclaim for ourselves all human potentials, including those unduly established as masculine, that is, those monopolized by men in order to enslave us more thoroughly. . . . For instance, violence: it's up to us to choose its forms and its goals. But violence is necessary against the violence of oppression. We want to be able to choose.[78]

A lesbian violence is not anti-life or pro-death, for it exhibits absolutely no equation between violence and destruction. *A lesbian creation and exercise of freedom, befriending and loving what is gentle and dear, is violence.* First, *a lesbian freedom is violence because it is dangerous to patriarchy, unrecoverable by it.* Secondly, *a lesbian freedom is violent in that it is dangerous to any aspect of myself that continues to function within the society of Mothers.* I want to lose all that is unfree, that reproduces the ideology of patriarchy. I want to live, in rupture with heterosexual virtue and its fragmentation of my existence, a genuine wholeness, harmony, and exuberance.

I passionately claim my subjectivity, my blood, my freedom, such that the image of women warriors who take up arms against the men and male institutions that oppress women is neither destructive nor unacceptable:

> They are possessed by such utter fury that they boil with anger tremble choke grind their teeth foam blaze rage and leap vomit run riot. They call them to account admonish them put a knife to their throats . . . acquaint them with all their grievances . . . ferment disturbances riots civil wars. . . .[29]

To men's monopoly of weapons, which has intensified male visibility historically and facilitated men's terrorization of women, I oppose a lesbian violence. We must take seriously, as Valerie Solanas indicates in the SCUM Manifesto, the idea of an organized violent uprising of women against men.[30] There is every reason to expand, carefully and strategically, the Amazon community which still exists, that is, to participate in the "community of women who perform tasks, together, that are viewed in patriarchal society as stereotypically male pursuits—defense, war, hunting, handling weapons, wearing and handling the accoutrements of war."[31] The claim that "an all-female army in patriarchal society is necessary for the liberation of women,"[32] as articulated by Susan Cavin, should be adopted wholeheartedly and immediately by women everywhere.

On a day-to-day basis, I must defend myself. Recognition of the devastating scope of men's war against women brings me, immediately and directly, to employ a lesbian violence whose means and ends are apart from those men have provided for me. Men's war, like men's concept of violence, fights to sustain the boundaries of men's territory, as identified variously with God, the state, and the heroic ego. A *lesbian war,* in accord with a lesbian creation and use of violence, *struggles to protect the absolutely essential boundaries of my body and to enable the formation of a lifeworld which embodies my priorities and particular loves.* Terror is made visible in the unfreedom of my body; terror is negated through my body's freedom.

III. Rape

Rape is that moment when a woman's life blood stops. My body is occupied and used by a man. My life is not my own. I become bloodless. The immediate experience of terror has always at least one possibility—my fragmentation and death.

Knowledge that rape happens, and a perspective on why such terrorism takes place, must be seen in the light of how rape may occur. Descriptive fidelity to the primary moments of a particular rape is a way of being true to the self which survives that change. Reflective description of the "how" of one particular rape forms the basis for a narrative that responds to men's terrorism of women. If the narrative depicts that terrorism in its immediacy, it also paints a

47

lesbian freedom, violence, and wholeness which constitute rape survival.

A woman never chooses to be raped. The rapist has no regard for women. He tells me who I am, he makes me exist according to the dictates of his will. In surviving rape, I exercise a radical choice to negate terror, to retain a blood, life, body, apart from the world of the rapist. In part due to a reprieve by the rapist, in part because of radical choices acted upon, I am still alive. I remember how I fought back and how I cared for my life.

Memories of the rape retain a power of interruption and invasion. The rapist's penis feels uncomfortable, grinding, thumping in and out. There is the sound of his feet on the floor, of his gun against my face. I have never been where, absolutely, I could not get out, where no matter what I did, physical or verbal, it did not work.

As I hear, once again, the sound of the rapist's feet on the floor, I am like the companion lovers who "agree upon the words that they do not want to forgo," calling it a trueness to self "to write one's life with one's blood."[33] Looking at my blood, I respond in narrative form to a moment in which my life blood was stopped.

About eleven o'clock on a sunny September morning, just as I am going outside to tend a potted plant, a man I saw earlier on the sidewalk reading neighborhood electric meters walks forcefully into my apartment and blocks the door. I scream loudly, stabbing at his neck with my gardening scissors. He takes his gun, holds it to my head and tells me to be quiet or he will blow my head off. He takes my glasses off, saying that he wants to see what I look like without them, then puts them back on. I look at his face so that I will know, in detail, the man who is to rape me—and am blindfolded. The neighbors seem not to be at home. No one responds.

His gun is at my head or, upon negotiation, on the floor from which he picks it up and puts it to my head at frequent intervals during the next hour and a half. I think how I can get downstairs, to the street, to my car, as he begins by robbing my money—fifteen dollars.

The heavy weight, smell, uncleanliness of the rapist, whose missionary position is coupled with his hands and arms around my head and neck, his gun poking at my skull, invades my person as he slobbers all over me and into my ears and mouth. I think of my friends—what advice would they give me? How would Marlena and Ingrid suggest I act to get out? Corky, Ruth, Denise, Judith and Gail, Rhonda, what would they do to stop this and stay alive? MaryLou is only down the street and Joyce nearby. Julie's gentle touch is here.

The rapist is like a bad movie, a disastrous rehearsal of enforced heterosexuality. Perhaps he does not really touch my body, for what he designates as my body is completely

49

distinct from how I perceive myself, from Julie's constant presence to me. A council of female advisors circles the bed, giving advice and summoning strong action. Julie is there; the rapist cannot touch the lesbian in me. But the rapist can shoot me at any time. I must make choices while forced to be unfree. The man is an experienced rapist, telling me in advance that if the phone rings it will not be answered. As steps are heard on the stairs outside, I am silenced by his renewed willingness to use his gun.

My breasts are judged too small by the rapist, and he continues anyway. He describes his penis, its shape, and size, along with what he considers the superior power and potency of a black man's penis. My tampon must be removed, he says. I feel horrible as the rapist forces his penis into me and grinds awhile. He has the nerve to analyze me in terms of my "pussy" and with regard to how he "fits." My attempts to constrict the vaginal opening so he cannot penetrate me come to a halt as he applies the gun. He is going to orgasm, and I must orgasm, on command, at exactly the same time. I refuse. He removes the blindfold, ordering me to look at his organ, stuck into me, and commanding me to say yes to all his comments concerning his perceptions of its shape and size. I try to see his face instead, to be able to identify him, but he prevents that by blindfolding me again. The rapist grinds up and down, frantically. It hurts. He pokes me with his gun, ordering me to orgasm. Finally, afraid, and angry and mortified, I make a few sounds. He ejaculates and remarks that my "orgasm" felt good to him.

I am repulsed. I will do anything to get rid of him, to shorten the time of the rape. Despite talk, negotiation, threats, and the exertion of physical strength until his arms and hands again come around my head and neck and I am poked with his gun—nothing works. I am covered with his hot sticky sperm. His body, immensely larger, heavier, longer than my own, comes down on me. He bangs at my sides, drills up and down like an oil well, and ejaculates again, remarking that he knows that I, a woman, cannot orgasm a second time as quickly as he. The grotesque and the dangerous converge. My council of female advisors gives excellent recommendations. They help keep going my spirits, determination, resolve to stop the rapist at every moment. I am reminded both that he may kill me and that he can never know, touch, invade, who I really am. The rapist resumes seesawing in and out of me. Now my body must function like a box that has one opening and admits a single instrument. He says I must orgasm again and applies his gun. I wonder whether he will fall asleep from exhaustion so I can pick up his gun and shoot him. I abhor him. Suddenly, he ejaculates. He has decided, he says, that I was probably tired and couldn't accompany him.

Having taken my money and occupied my body, the rapist now tries to invade the rest of my life. He asks an endless series of questions: What is my boyfriend like? Will I take the rapist for a ride in the car he saw me drive this morning? I finally convince him that such a ride would not be safe for him. He lectures me on why he, as a black man, is sexually "better" than a white man. He would

51

have liked to meet me elsewhere, after all, I am a "good girl" and he is a good man. He is so sorry to put me through this that he would like to instruct me on two matters: first, I should never, never touch myself—touching myself is the one thing I must never do. Instead, I should find a good man, someone like himself—could I "make love" to him again? Secondly, I must always keep my doors locked. I think, perhaps I am supposed to always stay inside a locked door and never go outside—and my whole life is to be as unfree as this rape? To get outside, I must unlock the door. I am covered with the smell, weight, stickiness of his body.

How to get out and how to get him out. Julie reassures me. I am still here. Under and apart from all this sliminess, I am still here. Now the rapist wants me to cook him dinner—beer and a steak. Fortunately, there are only vegetables in the refrigerator. He insists I must have more money. Still blindfolded, I am furious as he decides to play my piano while naked. He plays poorly—maybe the neighbors will hear and realize something is wrong. He recognizes that the piano is of some value and heatedly insists that I must have more money. I decide to tell him that the piano is from my parents who are dead. This catches his attention. He discourses on the sadness of death and proceeds to consider taking the stereo—until I convince him it is broken. The rapist uses his gun to get access to my identification and credit cards, whose contents he recites out loud.

Seemingly finished with his tasks, the rapist brushes his teeth and washes up, pocketing my toothbrush and toothpaste. For me, the problem remains how to get out and how to get him out. He plays with his gun at my head for what seems the longest time. I am threatened to not call the police, to not tell anyone, that he will come back. He wants to return. I fear whether he will leave me alive, for he seems unable to decide. Back and forth he walks around me with his gun. He tells me to stay still awhile, then to put on clothes and have dinner, not to leave the house, not to call anyone, that he wants to return. The gun continues to be poked at my head. The door closes and he has left.

I remove the blindfold, am afraid he is still outside, telephone Julie and decide to report to the hospital rape center and the police. The rapist's feel, his smell, stick to me.

As I listen to the narrative of my hidden veins, I see myself in the terror:

> ... healing must be sought
> in the blood of the wound itself.[34]

I am now visible in the rape, in the moment my blood was stopped. I look at my blood and touch a lesbian world that is free and open. Over and through myself, as through that world, flow the red waters of my veins.

A bath of flowers, kisses, hugs, anxiety and tears, begins the deeply flowing moment that brings me back into

trust, wholeness, and life. Three rounds of police interviews, a medical inspection of my body for evidence, even
fingerprinting of the piano keys are finished successfully
by midnight. Milkshakes in the early morning accompany
the move out of my apartment.

Whenever I think about the rape, I drink glasses and
glasses of water and take endless showers. The day after
the rape, I stay inside, hugging dearly the world that Julie
and I share. For some time, I shake whenever I go outside.

Friends become everything. I telephone and visit them
daily. They inspire me. Their care and concern accompanies
the continuance of my self and world.

Despite the presence of infinite amounts of identifying
evidence, the rapist is not found. He cannot be found, and
I must kill him and his world of terrorism—with the pen.
Olga Broumas's poem of the rape and killing of Imogene
Knode takes on an ever greater realism and necessity:

> I want
> this poem to be a weapon.
> I was a woman, gentle, and I did not live
> I call this poem to be a weapon.
> I give this poem authority to kill.[35]

The actionary writing, and the recorded actions, of Monique
Wittig's *les Guérillères* become for me, even more inten-
sively than before, the subject of a reflection whose aim is

. . . to write violence
outside the text
in another writing
threatening menacing
margins spaces intervals
without pause
action overthrow.[36]

Amidst an intense honesty and realism concerning the all-pervasive presence of men's terrorism, I find a strength whose buoyancy and resilience the rapist can never penetrate and before which he must, eventually, die.

After the rape, I must eat, work, and sleep as before. The rapist, who at gunpoint has gone through all my identification cards, knows where I work, the places that I frequent. Coming to school, I must often take public transportation, the rapist's probable employer. As I teach class, the door opens and closes unexpectedly. If I do errands for over half an hour, my nerves become raw and exhausted. A rawness of nerve recognizes with clarity the presence of violence. I have taught about rape for years. Nevertheless, I find it necessary to get rid of the bed, and the apartment in which the rape occurred. Even new sheets and pillowcases call forth vivid memories and I must throw everything out of the bed to be able to sleep.

Slowly, my body is touched, traced, and retraced, as I revive. In a sense, the rapist has not touched me, for he is unable to reclaim my body, life, world. I am not as he has tried to see me; no woman is. At the same time, I am afraid both to touch myself and to be touched, lest I am not all here. I am furious at the rapist and his world. Curves, angles, depths, spaces of my body are pieced back together, lovingly. The movements and expanse of my lesbian body, my friend's lesbian body, and our lifeworld, are painted anew. I want to touch and be touched...after all, I've made it and I am alive.

Several days later, I can finally feel all of myself while washing. My hands against my body, somewhat tenuously, assure me that all of me has survived.

Hidden veins become the waters that flow through me, painting blood red my passion to live in a lesbian strength, exuberance, and harmony. In the red of blood we, flowing deeply, trace a world of women that is gentle and dear, free and open. As Kathleen Barry writes, "They are not afraid of what we are *against.* They are afraid of what we are *for.* What we are for is so much more powerful than what we are against."[37]

IV. Effective Survival

Women often live through men's terrorism convinced that it forms an inevitable and unalterable dimension of women's lives. Women survive, at times, as individuals who hope for the possibility of a lifeworld where women's survival is no longer an issue. Yet, no matter how reassuring the survival of women as individuals may be, it is dangerously exhausting and ineffective. If women's survival does not radically subvert the objective structures of patriarchy—the ideology of male entitlement and the construct of women as beings to be empenised—women's unfreedom continues.

When women's survival is viewed in the context of women's self-defense, the goal becomes one of increasing women's possibilities for surviving men's ongoing terrorization. The use of arms is, in many instances, a most successful mode of defense, "In 150 cases where women threatened a would-be rapist with a gun or other weapon, almost 100 percent of the armed women succeeded in averting rape."[38] Yet, even the successful defensive use of arms is too late. All defensive strategies, no matter how successful, presuppose that male terrorism has again been experienced by yet another woman.

Men's terrorization of women need not, however, be endured at all. *Women's survival of men's terrorism becomes effective precisely when women make the possible actual: when women create, actively and collectively, a world of female friendship whose strength, harmony, and exuberance celebrate the similarities and differences of each individual.* Once women give first priority to the realization of a life together that is free and open, any entrapment within the structure of male terrorism is intolerable.

The priority that women's effective survival gives to the existence of my body and the body of my world, as I define them, marks that survival as specifically lesbian. I no longer regard myself as a woman, she who exists to be empenised, or as a Mother, she who produces for the sake of men. Women's effective survival accomplishes, rather, a radical subversion, both in its refusal to live within any aspect of the structures of patriarchy and in its creation of a world of life that is free and open. If a lesbian is "the rage of all women condensed to the point of explosion,"[39] so too is a lesbian the passion to live freely, the will to choose and to change the course of our blood. In a primordial sense, a lesbian is, "She Who carries herself in a bowl of blood."[40]

When priority is given to the freedom of my body in a world of female friendship, there is manifest the need for a collective female offense against men's terrorization of women. While all Amazonian actions subvert patriarchy—

> They say that they foster disorder in all its forms confusion troubles violent debates disarray upsets distrubances incoherences irregularities divergences complications disagreements discords clashes polemics discussions contentions brawls disputes conflicts debacles cataclysms disturbances quarrels agitation turbulence conflagration chaos...[41]

some actions may be more effective than others.

We must decide which actions are necessary for women's survival and freedom. If we are to live free from terror, the most effective actions are those that make impossible men's acts of terrorism. Men's terrorization of women is most effectively stopped before it can happen. In a world of female friendship and freedom, rape becomes a form of violation against which all women act to secure that it never exists again.

MOTHERHOOD:

THE ANNIHILATION OF WOMEN

I would like to affirm the rejection of motherhood on the grounds that motherhood is dangerous to women. If woman, in patriarchy, is she who exists as the womb and wife of man, every woman is by definition a mother: she who produces for the sake of men. *A mother is she whose body is used as a resource to reproduce men and the world of men, understood as the biological children of patriarchy and as the ideas and material goods of patriarchal culture.* Motherhood is dangerous to women because it continues the structure within which females must be women and mothers and, conversely, because it denies to females the creation of a subjectivity and world that is open and free.

An active rejection of motherhood entails the development and enactment of a *philosophy of evacuation.*[1] Identification and analysis of the multiple aspects of motherhood not only show what is wrong with motherhood, but also point to a way out. A philosophy of evacuation proposes women's collective removal of ourselves from all forms of motherhood. Freedom is never achieved by the mere inversion of an oppressive construct, that is, by seeing motherhood in a "new" light. Freedom is achieved when an oppressive construct, motherhood, is vacated by its members and thereby rendered null and void.

A small and articulate group of radical feminist and radical lesbian authors agree that motherhood is oppressive to women. Simone de Beauvoir's position in *The Second Sex,* that woman's "misfortune is to have been biologically destined for the repetition of life,"[2] is reaffirmed in her recent interviews: "I think a woman must not fall into the trap of children and marriage. Even if a woman wants to have children, she must think very hard about the conditions in which she will have to bring them up, because childbearing, at the moment, is real slavery."[3] Shulamith Firestone, following de Beauvoir, finds that, "the heart of woman's oppression is her childbearing and childrearing roles."[4] That woman's "reproductive function...is the critical distinction upon which all inequities toward women are grounded" is also asserted by Ti-Grace Atkinson at the beginning of the second wave of the women's liberation movement.[5] Monique Wittig writes that a female becomes a woman and a mother when she is defined first of all, and above all else, in terms of "the capacity to give birth (biology)."[6]

The claim that a direct connection exists between woman's oppression and her role as breeder within patriarchy entails the recognition that men impose a type of sexuality on women through the institution of motherhood. De Beauvoir agrees that "frigidity seems..., in the present state of malaise created by the power relationship between men and women, a reaction at least more prudent and more reasonable [than woman being trapped in sexuality] because it reflects this malaise and makes women less dependent on men."[7] Atkinson answers affirmatively the more specific question, "Do you still feel that sexual instincts would disappear if 'sexual intercourse' no longer served the function of reproduction?"[8] Andrea Dworkin states, "There is a continuum of phallic control. In the male system, reproductive and nonreproductive sex are both phallic sex."[9] Wittig holds that, "Sexuality is for us [lesbians] an inevitable battleground insofar as we want to get outside of genitality and of the sexual economy imposed on us by the dominant heterosexuality."[10] I engage in a philosophy of evacuation as a radical lesbian who questions, analyzes, and describes how motherhood is dangerous to women.

Speaking of motherhood as the annhilation of women does not disclaim either women's past or present as mothers. Women as mothers make the best of motherhood. Women are mothers because within patriarchy women have no choice except motherhood. Without the institution of motherhood women could and would live otherwise. Just as no single woman, or particular mother, is free in patriarchy, no group of token women, mothers in general, are free in patriarchy. Until patriarchy no longer exists, all females, as historical beings, must resist, rebel against, and avoid producing for the sake of men. Motherhood is not a matter of women's psychological or moral character. As an ideology by which men mark females as women, motherhood has nothing to do with a woman's selfishness or sacrifice, nurturance or nonviolence. Motherhood has everything to do with a history in which women remain powerless by reproducing the world of men and with a present in which women are expected to do the same. The central publication of the Soviet Women's Committee, for instance, writes, "Considering motherhood to be a woman's most important social function...."[11]

I am endangered by motherhood. In evacuation from motherhood, I claim my life, body, world, as an end in itself.

I. Where Do Children Come From?

The question "Where do babies come from?" is frequently dismissed with a laugh, or cut short by recourse to scientific authority. In present-day discourse, both God's prescience and the stork are generally thought to be adequate responses. A satisfactory and "progressive" explanation is found in a scientific account of the union of egg and sperm. The appeal to science is misleading, however, for it ignores and conceals the social intercourse that first brings men and women together either directly, by means of physical copulation, or indirectly, through the use of medical technology.[12] The question "Where do babies come from?" might be approached more appropriately through the social and historical circumstances in which conception takes place: *Children come from patriarchal (male) sexuality's use of woman's body as a resource to reproduce men and the world of men.*

The scientific explanation of where children come from avoids placing conception within the continuum of social power relationships that constitute motherhood: heterosexual intercourse, pregnancy, and childraising. Compulsion marks every aspect of the motherhood continuum: the mandatory heterosexuality imposed on women by men is thought "natural"; pregnancy is viewed as a biological "fact"; obligatory childraising by women is considered entirely "normal."[13]

Seduction and pregnancy, for instance, are remarkably similar: both eroticize women's subordination by acting out and deepening women's lack of power.[14]

> Male instinct can't help ITself; women need IT either because of their sexiness or their maternal instinct. IT, the penis, is big; IT, the child, is large. Woman's body is made for IT. Women's bodies have the right fit, or proportions. Women ask for IT, want IT. IT's a maturing experience in her becoming a woman. She takes IT. No real harm is done.

In seduction and pregnancy the power imbalance between men and women assumes the appearance of sexual difference, regardless of whether such activities are "affectionate" or "brutal."

> If women didn't want IT, IT wouldn't happen. Therefore, women must choose IT. Since many choose IT, IT must be part of their nature.[15]

I am defenseless within the motherhood continuum.

IT, "male instinct," passes through heterosexual intercourse to become the IT of motherhood. In motherhood, IT, male sexuality as a man-made social power construct, marks females with ITself. IT compels women to ITself: to male sexuality and its consequences, namely, birthing and raising men and the world of men. Children come from IT, from male-defined, male-dominated social intercourse. IT names ITself as "virility": belonging to, characteristic of a man; the power of procreation, especially for sexual intercourse; the masculine member, the generative organs; force, energy, drive considered typically masculine; to pursue, to hunt.[16] Virility comes from *vir,* which in Latin means "man." Women's "misfortune is to have been biologically destined for the repetition of life"[17] precisely because ITs power, force, energy, drive appropriates women's biological possibility in order to produce ITself. IT pursues ITs own continuation, silencing my questions: Is IT needed? Is IT desired? IT pursues ITs own evolution, constituting motherhood as a given, as compulsory for women, a danger to women.

▽   ▽   ▽

One might object that children have not always come from patriarchal (male) sexuality's use of woman's body as a resource to reproduce men and the world of men. An appeal may even be made to a time in which motherhood is said to have had nothing to do with men's appropriation of women's bodies.

Çatal Hüyük, in particular, has been cited as "a very early urban culture which appears to have venerated women's activities, especially their procreative ones."[18] The Neolithic goddess at Çatal Hüyük who is claimed to clearly express "female experience and power" and the presence of "a positive female religious role" is described by Anne Barstow:

> Around 6200 B.C. the first goddess appears, in plaster outline on the wall, her legs spread wide, giving birth; below her, rows of plaster breasts, nipples painted red, are molded over animal skulls or jaws which protrude through the nipples. Already at her first appearance she is the deity of both life and death.[19]

Further examination of the context in which the Çatal Hüyük goddess appears shows, however, that care must be taken not to misconstrue the historical situation of women as mothers in early human culture. Females at Çatal Hüyük are represented exclusively in terms of maternal organs and attributes. Squatting in childbirth, usually with raised arms and legs, women are defined by their engagement in childbirth or, sometimes, pregnancy.[20] The female's head is less defined than the rest of her body, and often is not shown at all.[21] Synonymous with women's function as mother and maintainer of life at Çatal Hüyük is women's early death: "The average adult age [at Çatal Hüyük] was 34.3 years for men, 29.8 years for women."[22] The significantly shorter life-span of women at Çatal Hüyük demonstrates that although a culture may "venerate" woman as mother, it may fail to empower individual women who spend much of their lives giving birth.

Examination of the context in which the Çatal Hüyük goddess appears makes evident, moreover, that the goddess was not alone. The goddess is regularly shown with the phallus: Neolithic figurines found as the cult inventory of shrines are "nearly always accompanied by an array of broken-off stalagmites or stalactites... many of the natural concretions suggest breasts or phalli."[23] Similar groupings of Neolithic female statuettes with amulets in the form of phalli are found in the Mesopotamian lowlands, at Chagar Bazar, and in Southern Iran, at Tepe Guran.[24] Even in the earlier Paleolithic period, the goddess is frequently accompanied by the phallus: "the clay models of a female bison [are] followed by a male placed against a projecting rock in a small chamber at the end of a long narrow passage in the Tuc d'Audoubert.... In a recess nearby were pieces of clay in the form of a phallus."[25]

Evidence concerning women as mothers at Çatal Hüyük does not support the claim that motherhood once existed outside patriarchy. The Çatal Hüyük goddess is usually surrounded by men more powerful than herself. She is often shown giving birth to a son, represented even in infancy as a bull, ram, or other horned animal.[26] The son's social status surpasses immediately that of the goddess, as is exemplified by the Çatal Hüyük leopard statue: "the goddesses stand behind the animals, whereas the boy god rides on it."[27] At Çatal Hüyük, as at many Paleolithic and Neolithic sites, the female power of life and death is consistently accompanied by the larger than life image of the male power of "wild life and death":

> As a symbol of male fertility an aurocks bull or a large ram was more impressive than man himself and the power of wild life and death was suitably symbolized in the leopard, the largest and fiercest wild animal in the region; in the destructive ferocity of the boar or in the impressive spectacle of flocks of Griffon vultures.[28]

Women's freedom is to be sought not by reclaiming the forms of motherhood that appear at Çatal Hüyük, but by engaging in an evacuation from motherhood in all its manifestations. That women at Çatal Hüyük were defined as mothers does not mean that such a definition was either natural or necessary. Indeed, without such an all-encompassing definition of woman's being, the goddess of Çatal Hüyük might have existed otherwise. *I separate from the deification and exploitation of women as womb and mother.*[29]

II. The Representation

The question remains: "Where do children come from?" If children are, and perhaps always have been, produced by IT, by male sexuality as a man-made social power construct: How does male sexuality appropriate women's biological possibility in order to reproduce ITself?

Motherhood is constituted by male sexuality's use of woman's body to represent ITself to ITself. As such, motherhood is a paradigmatic instance of men's creation of representational thinking and of men's appropriation of the ''world'' by means of representational thought.

Representational thinking does not mean the production of a picture, copy, or imitation *of* the world. Representational thinking means, rather, to conceive and grasp the world *as* picture.[30] In representational thinking, man manipulates, pursues, and entraps the world in order to secure it as picture. Man brings into play his unlimited power for the calculating, planning, and molding of all things.[31] By conceiving and grasping the world as picture, he gives the measure and draws up the guidelines for everything that is.[32] He creates and determines what is real, and what is not. Not only is the man who has made the picture already in the picture, he is that which he pictures to himself. If man were to acknowledge himself as the picture, he would destroy himself as he who conceives and grasps the world as picture. Only by maintaining a privileged stand outside the picture can man claim to be the creator, and not the object, of the activity of representation. Withdrawn from representation as the representer, he enters into the picture as ''the incalculable,'' ''the gigantic.''[33]

The object of representational thought is allowed to be only insofar as it can be overpowered—manipulated, pursued, entrapped—by representational thought. Once conceived and grasped as picture, the object is said to call forth, to provoke, the specific way in which it is pictured and the activity of picturing as such.[34] The object can, indeed, must repeat itself exactly as it has been thought. It must even claim to establish, maintain, and justify its objectification. Its sole "activity" is reproductive: the reiteration and reinforcement of itself as picture.

Reproductive thinking generates, unavoidably and of necessity, an ideology that is reproductive: motherhood. Athena is born from the head of Zeus alone; children are born from the head of man alone.[35] Athena springs fully armed from the head of Zeus; a child springs from the head of its father, fully adorned with the markings of patriarchy. Zeus sees his world in his full-grown offspring; man pictures his world in his children who soon will be adults. Even if the child is female, man incorporates the female into his world as picture. The man with the child in his head, with the child as image in his head, represents himself to himself in the child he has made. In contrast, Athena's mother, Metis, cannot be manipulated, pursued, trapped. She cannot be bound, secured, by man's representational thought. Athena's mother, children's mothers, are not.

In representational thought, woman is made pregnable [from *prehendere,* Latin for "to take"], understood in its literal sense as vulnerable to capture, taken. She is compelled to have man's child, to reproduce throughout her world of experience men's thoughts, words, actions. She must reproduce the life of the species, that is, man and his immortality. Captured by representational thinking, woman can never be genuinely pregnant [*pre-gnas,* akin to *gignere,* to produce]: she cannot produce her own life and world. Woman as what-in-men's-eyes-she-seems-to-be[36] is invisible, except insofar as her body is used by man to reproduce himself and his world. Motherhood passes through the mind of a man who does not see woman's body as her body. Throughout the motherhood continuum of heterosexual intercourse, pregnancy, and child raising, woman as what-I-am-in-my-own-eyes is not.

Key to the specific mode of representation that defines motherhood, including the articulation of woman's sexuality within the confines of motherhood, is male sexuality's setting of the bounds within which life and death are to be recognized. Man, the representer, assumes a greater-than-human power over life and death. Man, the representer, fixates on life and death as the central defining moments, or parts, of one's life. Man's representation of life and death reduces woman's body to a lifeless instrument, even when her body is a carrier of life and death. The manner in which man represents life and death precludes the experience of what is always already given: the continuity and discontinuity of an individual life, the strength and power of ongoing action in the world, the authentic subjectivity of the woman who is *as* she is.

While man is giving birth to himself, woman dies. *I, bound to the representation of woman as mother, leave that representation behind: evacuation to another way of thinking, to a productive empowering of the female who has been both woman and mother.*

III. The Mark

The question "Where do children come from?" may be answered in terms of that form of consciousness, the representation, and that form of existence, the mark, by which patriarchal (male) sexuality justifies the appropriation of women's bodies as a resource to reproduce men and the world of men.[37] Interpretation of the representation and the mark portray, when taken together, the social intercourse that is motherhood. A philosophy of evacuation proposes that from which women must collectively remove ourselves: patriarchal thinking, the representation, and patriarchal existence, the mark.

The mark imposed by patriarchy on the bodies of all women compels all women to exist as mothers. The mark of motherhood inscribes the domination of men into woman's body, making motherhood appear as a natural

73

phenomenon. Yet, motherhood is not a natural phenomenon and mothers do not exist as a natural group. On the contrary, female biological possibilities are first "naturalized" by men as women's specific difference and then claimed as the reason for the existence of motherhood.[38] Through such "naturalization," the female's biological possibility to give birth is made to appear as the intrinsic cause of woman's place in motherhood and as the origin of woman's social, economic, and political place in the world. The female's biological capacity to bear a child becomes the defining characteristic of all women.

Marking focuses on isolated fragments of the female body.[39] Such fragments, vagina, breasts, etc., are marked with a significance that is presumed to be intrinsic, eternal, and to characterize the whole of the female body. Forms of activity and character traits termed "natural" to women are then deduced from the marking imposed on the body fragments.

The closer a mark is to the body, the more indelibly it is associated with the body and the more the individual as a whole is pursued, hunted, trapped.[40] In the case of woman, the mark has absolute permanence, for woman's entire body, and the body of her world, is marked: MOTHER. The permanence of the mark is the sign of the permanence of the male domination that marks all women as mothers.

The object marked, woman as mother, experiences the mark as pain. The inscription of the mark of motherhood on women's bodies is never without pain—the pain of not "owning" our bodies, the pain of physical injury, the pain of being compelled to never produce a life or world of our own. Pain [from Greek *poinē,* punishment, penalty, payment] is the punishment, the penalty we must pay, for being marked by men as woman and mother. Pain has nothing to do with what we do, that is, our success or failure at being good, well-informed, or willing mothers. Pain is a sign that we, as women, are endangered by men who mark us. *If and when* the pain of the mark is not successfully "naturalized" by men, that is, is not or does not remain imprinted on females as belonging to our nature either physiologically or psychologically, we attempt to evade pain. Our pain breaks through the force of the mark. We do not endure the pain. We do not put up with the mark. We avoid, resist, the mark. We neither need nor desire the mark. We will get out of the mark. The immense amount of pain that marking entails is both an experience that accompanies the mark of motherhood and an experience that can lead to the end of the mark of motherhood.

Among those institutions created by marking, the institution of motherhood is unique: there is no other institution in which so many persons can be destroyed by the mark, and yet, a sufficient supply of persons to be marked remains. In all other forms of war, attrition eventually threatens the supply of persons who can be marked and thereby limits the activity of marking, at least for a time. The mark of motherhood is distinctive in that one of its by-products is the regeneration of more females to be marked as women and mothers.

Outside the social power relationship within which marking occurs, the mark does not exist.[41] Outside patriarchy, the mark of motherhood cannot even be imagined.

▽   ▽   ▽

Women's daily life within patriarchy is shaped by the mark of motherhood. The genitalia and stomach are among the primary fragments of the female body which are so marked, as is woman's body as a whole.

Cut, carved, and literally burned into women's bodies are both the conditions under which our bodies will be open to the world, i.e., when, where, and to which individual men, and the world to which our bodies will be open, i.e., the world of men. From the mark of virginity to that of genital mutilation, our genitalia are marked: MOTHER.

In all modern culture, the marking of women's genitalia is indelible, permanently closing us to alternative decisions within patriarchy, as well as to the decision to create other possible and non-patriarchal worlds. On 42nd Street in New York City, movies on excision are featured attractions.[42] Our genitalia are marked to give us "worth": the smaller the artificial passage made by genital mutilation, the greater our "value," the higher our brideprice. Without the operation we cannot get a husband. We are "worthless."[43] Our genitalia are marked to improve heterosexual intercourse: Dr. James Burt, a Dayton, Ohio, gynecologist, "reconstructs" women for "better" intercourse. For a fee of $1,500, he surgically tightens the vaginal opening of female patients to bring the vagina and the clitoris closer together.[44] To make us desire marriage our genitalia are marked: "Only when they [young girls] are ready to procreate is it [the clitoris] removed—and once it is they feel deprived. Their desire then is concentrated in one place only and they promptly get married."[45] To regulate "madness" our genitalia are marked: "Circumcision, which...is confined to the clitoris, sets a barrier to the mad life of the girls," to the "lasciviousness" of eight year old females.[46] Marking is used as "social protection" against teenage heterosexual intercourse and pregnancy: "Why should not the United States and Europe be investigating the possibilities of hygenic experimentation with female circumcision as a social safeguard" from "teen sex" and "teen parenthood."[47] Marking as a "social safeguard" against rape: "infibulation is necessary to protect women from being raped."[48] Or, to "protect" the family.[49] One hundred percent of the female population of Somalia, Sudan, and Dijbouti,[50] sixty-five million women in those areas of Africa from which such estimates are available,[51] and increasing numbers of females in France, Norway, and Australia experience genital mutilation as the mark of motherhood.[52] Pain, illness, and death accompany the mark that initiates us into motherhood.[53]

The mark of motherhood imprints on us patriarchal (male) sexuality. It cuts, carves, and literally burns into our bodies men's "needs," men's "desires":

> A virgin body... what he alone is to take and to pene-
> trate seems to be in truth created by man. And more,
> one of the ends sought by all desire is the using up of
> the desired object, which implies its destruction.[54]

From the idea of virginity to the act of genital mutilation, the mark of motherhood controls where we may walk in the world of men, and that we must walk only in the world of men.

Stamped, firmly imprinted on women's bodies, is the emblem that our bodies have been opened to the world of men: the shape of the pregnant woman's stomach. From conception to abortion, acts which are biologically different and yet symbolically the same, our stomachs are marked: MOTHER.

In present-day patriarchal society, the marking impressed on woman's stomach is man's proof of his virility, that he can reproduce himself. When the mark remains on women's stomachs from conception to the birth of an infant, male virility not only can, but does, reproduce itself. In contrast, when the mark remains imprinted on our stomachs from conception to the abortion of a fetus, male virility can, but does not—yet—reproduce itself. Either the time is judged as not right—yet, or the right time has passed by—already. When abortion is permitted in patriarchy, either officially or unofficially, there need not be an immediate and direct link between conception and the birth of an infant. There must, however, be an indirect link between male virility which can reproduce itself and male virility which does reproduce itself. The right time must eventually be found such that man both can and does reproduce himself, either by means of biological children or through the material goods and ideas of patriarchy. Indeed, within patriarchy the fact that abortion may sometimes be permitted does not make abortion a genuinely free choice, for women have no alternative but abortion if we are already impregnated and do not want to reproduce. Nor does the right to abortion make motherhood voluntary, for a woman in patriarchy cannot abort, or do away with, the mark of motherhood. The right to abortion in patriarchy cannot, in principle, recognize that women may choose abortion because we will not reproduce men and the world of men, because we will not be mothers.

The woman who does not remove the mark from her stomach, who does not have an abortion, may be killed: on the West Bank one such Arab woman a week is found "poisoned or burned to death and the murder is made to look accidental."[55] Women who survive an initial decision to not remove the mark from our stomachs, to not have an abortion, in defiance of the traditions of male virility, may be persecuted as nonvirgins and unmarried mothers.[56] Yet, the women who do remove the mark from our stomachs, who abort, may also die. Five thousand women a year are estimated to die in Spain and Portugal alone as a result of complications arising from illegal abortions.[57] In Latin America, abortion causes twenty percent to fifty percent of all maternal deaths.[58] Complications from illegal abortions account for four percent to seventy percent of maternal deaths in the hospitals of developing countries.[59] A woman undergoing a properly performed abortion has six times less risk of death from complications than a woman having a child.[60] In childbirth our bodies as a whole are stamped with the mark of pain, terror, and possible death.

To speak of birth without violence is to ignore the violence of childbirth.[61] The most frequent cause of death of women is childbirth:[62]

In a number of developing countries...maternal mortality rates in excess of five hundred per hundred thousand live births are by no means exceptions. Rates of over one thousand per hundred thousand have been reported in parts of Africa.[63]

In the areas with the highest maternal mortality, i.e., most of Africa, West, South, and East Asia, about half a million women die from maternal causes every year.[64]

Age-specific death rates for women rise sharply between the ages of twenty and thirty in many countries, where women often have less chance than men of surviving from fifteen to forty-five years of age.[65]

Already, as female children, women as a whole are marked—"undesirable." College students in the United States, for instance, favor what amounts to a decrease in female births, with the overall ratio of girls to boys desired designated as 100:116.[66] In addition, "from sixty-six to ninety-two percent of men have been found to want an only child to be a boy..., and from sixty-two to eighty percent prefer a first child to be a boy," a chilling thought as the United States, like Western Europe, moves toward zero growth.

As female fetuses, women as a whole are stamped "to be aborted." A recent Chinese report, for example, shows that when sex determination tests were performed on one hundred fetuses for the sole purpose of determining the fetuses' gender, twenty-nine of the forty-six female fetuses, but only one of the fifty-three male fetuses, were aborted.[67]

As female infants, women as a whole are marked "dead." Men, rather than regulate men and men's use of women, claim that because there is not enough food, resources, etc., "female fertility" must be controlled by the elimination of women.[68] From the Athens of antiquity to the present, infanticide has been, largely and for the most part, femicide.[69]

Women as mothers are marked: dead. Man the marker continues with himself, his sons, his mark.

IV. The Society of Mothers

Man remains with his representation and his mark. Women need not remain. The representation and the mark, and not existing females, are integral to motherhood. If and when the representation and the mark of motherhood can be affixed to something other than the female body, women may not exist at all.

The society of mothers, comprised of all women within motherhood, is dangerous to all its members.[70] The society of mothers continues, by definition, the ideology and institution of motherhood as oppressive to women. The motherhood lived out by the society of mothers is the annihilation of women.

The forms of annihilation by which the society of mothers is endangered are multiple. Whenever motherhood involves men's representation and marking of females, motherhood entails the death of a world in which women are free, and motherhood may entail the physical death and non-existence of women as mothers and as female infants. In the contemporary ideology and institution of motherhood, women's annihilation may also be brought about when men represent and mark objects from the domain of the sciences and technology of reproduction to reproduce men and the world of men, such that the class, women as mothers, has no further use function, and thus, need no longer exist. In a patriarchal context, even the production of females by parthenogenesis need not alter the social and historical circumstances of the society of mothers into which such females would be born.[71] Men may or may not continue to impose patriarchal (male) sexuality on women. Regardless of whether men relate to women in explicitly sexual modes, women may still be kept in a service function as the society of mothers.

The representation and mark of motherhood claim not just the surface, but the whole of women, such that the society of mothers not only reproduces, but often defends, the patriarchal world of men: "Confined to their cities the mothers were no longer separate, free, complete individuals and they fused into an anonymous collective consciousness."[72] So strong is the force of the representation and mark that the society of mothers often maintains its own repetition:

> They developed a whole 'new' culture in which nothing could escape analogy to their own engenderment. They were fascinated by myths about rotundity, germination, earth and fructification of trees. Then the mothers began fabricating representations of themselves.... This brought about the procession of pregnant goddesses that history has since known.[73]

In the production of the son for the father, in the production of goods for the father, for the benefit of the son, we are not our bodies, we are not ourselves. A means to men's ends, never an end in ourselves, we are selfless, world-less, annihilated. *The experience of our servitude takes seriously our danger and holds, firmly and strongly, to the conviction that we must get out of motherhood.*

V. Priorities and Alternatives

To show how motherhood, in its many forms, is danger-ous to women is also to suggest how women may get out of motherhood. *Central to a philosophy of evacuation from motherhood is the primacy of women's daily lives and the power of our possible, and sometimes actual, collective actions.* In breaking free from motherhood, I no longer focus on birth and death as the two most important moments of my life. I give priority, rather, to that which is always already given: my life and my world. I—my activities, body, sexuality—am articulated by my actions and choices which, apart from patriarchy, may be made in the openness of freedom. I no longer give a primacy to that which I have reproduced. New modes of thinking and existing emerge. I, as an individual female, and we, as the community of all females, lay claim to our own freely chosen subjectivities, to the priorities and alternatives we create as our own.

The evacuation from motherhood does not simply seek to alter motherhood as it exists currently. Its focus is not specifically the development of alternative means of inter-course, pregnancy, or child care.[74] Women who use artifi-cial insemination and whose children have no known father and women who live as lesbian mothers clearly challenge, but need not break with, the ideology and institution of motherhood. Each of these alternatives is significant for women's survival within patrarchy, but none is sufficient for women's effective survival, that is, for the creation of a female's self-chosen, non-patriarchal, existence. A precondition for women's effective survival may be established, instead, by a female's power to not have children. A decision not to have children may be made, not because a female's biological capacity causes the ideology of motherhood, but because:

1. To not have children opens a time-space for the priority of claiming my life and world as my own and for the creative development of radically new alternatives.

2. The biology from which a child is born does not determine or control the course of that child's life. Females and males, younger and older, create the shapes of our lives through our actions.

3. Women who wish to be with younger females or males can do so collectively, with others of similar interests, or individually, through adoption.

At present, and for several thousands of years past, women have conceived, borne, and raised multitudes of children without any change in the conditions of our lives as women. In the case that all females were to decide not to have children for the next twenty years, the possibilities for developing new modes of thought and existence would be almost unimaginable.

The necessary condition for women's evacuation from motherhood is the claiming of our bodies as a source. Our bodies are not resources to be used by men to reproduce men and the world of men while, at the same time, giving death to ourselves. If necessary, women must bear arms, but not children, to protect our bodies from invasion by men.[75] For our effective survival, women's repetitive reproduction of patriarchy must be replaced by the creative production of ourselves. In particular, the areas of food, literacy, and energy sources and supplies for women must be examined anew.

Women's hunger is one of the specific conditions affecting the possibility for men's continuing success in representing and marking women as mothers. In the current patriarchal economy, women are the majority of the world's farmers, but women, on a global basis, do not have access to sufficient food to feed ourselves.[76] Nor do women have access to the money necessary to purchase food: women living in poverty constitute twelve percent of the total, world-wide, female population and seventy-five percent of all people living in poverty.[77]

Women's literacy is the second specific condition that enhances the possibility for men's continuing success in maintaining the ideology and institution of women as mothers. Women have insufficient access to the basics of literacy, that is, reading, writing, and simple arithmetic. From a global prespective, women are two-thirds of the illiterate people of the world.[78] In almost all countries, "girls already begin school in fewer numbers than boys; on the average, the difference even at the start of school is ten to twenty percent. By the time higher education is reached, the ratio between boys and girls is at least two to one, but in many cases more."[79] The education gap between men and women is growing throughout the developing world.[80] Even in industrialized societies, women have no access to determining which areas of research are the most urgent, or what constitutes an education.

Energy sources and supplies for women are a third area that undermines women's endeavors to break free of motherhood. In many villages in Africa and Asia, women work about three hours per day more than men because women are expected to gather the food, water, and fuel necessary for survival.[81] Technological information on alternative means of energy is usually not made available to these women, any more than it is to most women in industrialized countries. In all societies, women's non-control of energy sources and supplies necessary to our survival keeps us in subordination to men.

Female-defined access to food, education, and energy forms a necessary condition for women's collective evacuation from motherhood, for such access claims as a source the whole of our bodies and world. To get out of the reproduction of motherhood, females of all ages must work together to establish alternatives that express and fulfill our current needs and desires. As females who engage in evacuation from motherhood, we shape the whole of ourselves and our world in the present of our own lifetimes.

THE NAMING OF DIFFERENCE:
TRUTH AND FEMALE FRIENDSHIP

I took my lyre and said:

*Come now, my heavenly
tortoise shell: become
a speaking instrument*

Sappho[1]

Female friendship—liquid, freely flowing, watery and damp—the aqueous. The fluidity of female friendship first emerges with Artemis, goddess of the springs, named "a great spring" and "the source of all the waters."[2] Yet, soon after its naming, the aqueous is suppressed. Love and friendship between women, arising apart from men, become dominated by the ideal of male bonding in Greek antiquity. By the time of Socrates, bonds between men are tied to a logocentrism based on the principle of identity and its correlates, the principle of difference and the principle of equality. The principle of identity, created by the very men it governs, regulates all dealings between men and entails, of necessity, an ethic of domination and a metaphysic of sight. Within this logocentrism, the intimacy of the aqueous is invisible. The world of women, its passion, beauty, and fluid tones, is manifest only as identical to, different from, or equal to, a world constructed by men.

Yet, although torn apart in its tissue by men's logocentric vision, the world of female friendship has maintained an ethics of care and a metaphysics of touch. Apart from the ties that bind men, *a fundamental ontological rupture is effected by women.*[3] Within the ambiance of touch, and in the coincidence of touch and tongue, women enact another naming of our friendship.

▽   ▽   ▽

Pulling and lifting her torn skin off, layer by layer, a friend invokes Sappho, "give m/e by thousands the fingers that allay the wounds, give m/e the lips, the tongue the saliva which draw one into the slow sweet country from which one cannot return."[4] Even at the entrance to this country of touching and tasting, elicited above by Monique Wittig, we experience a tactile metaphysic. We discover ourselves, our friends and their worlds in the unending surprise of bodily presence.

Embodied and alive, we find ourselves outside the patriarchal history of the domination of vision, of its division of the universe into subjects and objects, the seer and the seen. No longer subordinated to the subject who establishes our identity in relation to his own and then validates our behavior as correct, we cease to be seen as objects. No longer obliged by man to say what he wants to hear, we refuse that feminine discourse which he has created.

Now, fingertips and lips, a friend touches the world, her friends, herself. Sight and speech are folded into the intimacy of the tactile, for everything condenses and rarifies with everything else, springing from and falling into the aqueous.

▽   ▽   ▽

The slow sweet country of touch stretches out apart from the principles of male logocentrism. The objectification effected by a seer outside and above the field of experience is undercut by a lively awareness of multiple interconnections. Left behind is the metaphysic of vision in which there predominates the principle of identity. There the seer exists as absolutely identical with himself and, in agreement with Nicholas of Cusa's formulation, "as nothing other than himself and as nothing other than the world," as admitting "no difference, no otherness whatsoever."³ Ignored is the male-defined principle of difference. Although the seer, from within his solipsism, may construct woman as "the other," he remains blind to his limits. He can prescribe an irreducible difference between "the sexes," or posit woman as his "twin" essence, only by missing women's existence altogether. Anxious at any possible loss of his univocity, the seer may even chance upon the ideal of equality. Yet, only the seer can believe that he can place woman safely next to himself as "the same."

The principle of identity and its correlates, the principle of difference and the principle of equality, remain in the stilled sky of the Platonic ideal. The logocentrism of Western logic, legislated by men, institutes an order that pretends to govern a world it does not see, hear, or touch.

The apartness of female friendship emerges, however, with the question posed most succinctly by Hélène Cixous, "What would become of logocentrism, of the great philosophical systems, of world order in general, if the rock upon which they founded their church were to crumble?"[6] The felt emergence of meaning within the context of lived experience displaces the assignment of meaning from the perspective of distance. Shedding the debris of the logocentric ideal, female friendship washes away the principle of identity and its correlates. The spinal valley,[7] touched by the friends, dips slowly into the great spring.

▽   ▽   ▽

In aqueous celebrations, women enact another meaning of our friendship. Our bodies become anew the fabric into which objects and words are woven.[8] Transforming and transformed by our multiple modes of embodiment, meanings shift, words coalesce. Words are then indistinguishable from our worlds of experience; names are then inseparable from ourselves. Living names have a physiognomy that creates and sustains a world of female friendship, for we adopt toward such words, as toward one another, an abiding solicitude and care. Bodies radiant with infinite symbols of the world celebrate, in sensitive gestural language, our being together.

At home in the coincidence of touch and tongue, friends free ourselves from the male logic and domination which have endeavored to make invisible our togetherness. We are freed by naming the limits of logocentrism. Naming frees, as in the story of "Rumpelstiltskin" who, when named by the queen, became so angry that "he stamped with his right foot so hard that it went into the ground above his knee; then he seized his left foot with both his hands in such a fury that he split in two, and there was an end of him."[9]

The event of gestural language forms already the beginning of a new naming of our friendship. The possibilities for our naming are, as Olga Broumas indicates, as varied as the friends ourselves:

> A woman-made language would
> have as many symbols for pink / light-filled / holy as
> the Eskimo does
> for snow.[10]

Friends feel the presence of those "syllables nestled in bones," syllables which "continue to speak themselves out of a need to be heard."[11] We continue floating, sipping, flowing in the spring in celebration of an originary naming of our friendship.

I. The Eclipse of Female Friendship

Although freed by naming the limits of the metaphysic of sight, we retain in memory the suppression of our friendship. The eclipse of female friendship, dominated by the ideal of male bonding in Greek antiquity, has lasted from the time of Socrates through the modern period.

93

Recollection of this brutal eclipse enables friends to dissolve its still lingering shadows. Such recollection may also empower us to remember ourselves.

With Socrates there is an "exploitation of the Athenian homosexual ethos as a basis of metaphysical doctrine and philosophical method."[12] An ethic and metaphysic of male bonding is developed with definite implications for daily life: "to an extent unparalleled in any other culture, homosexuality was rationalized into a philosophic and educational ideal and thereby, in theory at least, came to be seen as a state-building and order-maintaining force."[13]

How male homosexuality became the ideal of the ruling group in Greek society, founding an ethic, a metaphysic, and a politic, is explained most succinctly by Socrates' observation: "beauty is the only one, of those things... 'attracting eros,' which can be directly perceived by the senses, so that the sight of something beautiful affords by far the most powerful and immediate access we have to the world of Being."[14] Here sight seeks the identity of the seer with the seen. In the erotic bonds between men, each is for the other a means toward the end, the world of Being. Both individuals seek to resemble "something outside and above them."[15] Their vision is no longer fixed on "that which is mixed with darkness, on coming into being and passing away," but on those unchanging things that are illuminated by the sun: the intellection of that which *is*.[16] Male homosexuality becomes the ideal precisely because it claims to achieve, through a metaphysic of vision and a primacy of the principle of identity, a special relation to truth.

Male homosexuality in Greek society is viewed as the product "not of the reciprocated sentiment of equals, but of the pursuit of those of lower status by those of higher status."[17] Pursuit, competition, and capture typify the Greek male *eros* which, when used figuratively [*eran*], can mean victory, money, power. The "exceptional" man is he who, through his success in the closely connected activities of lover, athlete, and warrior, comes to stand over he who is "lesser."[18]

Yet, all Greek men are considered to be in some way noble. And men, only, can be noble. Plato writes, "woman . . . is a twofold, and more than a twofold problem, in proportion as her native disposition is inferior to man's."[19] The eros of Greek male bonding thereby asserts its ethic of domination over women.

Women are excluded from the world of significant relationships and from the marketplace of philosophic discourse: "When Pericles says that the best women arc those of whom the least is heard, whether in praise or blame (Thucydides II, 45, 1), he is certainly expressing the prevailing opinion among Athenians and among the Greeks as a whole."[20] Women do not participate in the political life of the classical period. In fact, women usually live shut off from the outside world in the women's chamber [*gynaikeion*], a room not unlike the cave in Plato's *Republic*.[21] Woman, she who is by nature without truth, lives, without speech, in the realm of darkness and shadow.

In Athenian life, women are, moreover, always excluded from eros.[22] Eros presides solely in relations between men. Eros, eclipsing his mother, Aphrodite, provides to men alone the means for the ascent from that which is perceived directly by the senses to a vision of the True, the Good, and the Beautiful.[23] Aphrodite, in contrast, must witness not the beauty, but the violation, of women. Her primary domain is heterosexual intercourse where, as we find in Attic vase painting, the woman is almost invariably: "in a 'subordinate' position, the man 'dominant': the woman bent over or lying back or supported, the man upright or on top."[24] Aphrodite must endure the depiction of women as the most generally penetrable of all beings. Whereas classical Greek representations of male homosexual fellation are absent, there are recurrent scenes of "a youth cramming his penis into a woman's mouth or a man threatening a woman with a stick and forcing her to 'go down on' him."[25]

▽   ▽   ▽

At the height of the Athenian ethic of domination there first appears in the Western philosophic tradition the paradigm whose multiple variations are to contribute to the ongoing eclipse of women and female friendship: the androgyne. Within the androgynic paradigm, the moon, tides, and the deepest of springs, that is, the world of female friendship, become shadows which are forced into darkness. Eclipsed by the brutal light of the sun, the creative power and fullness of the female world is nearly erased.

The androgyne, from the very first, reinforces the Greek ideal of male bonding. The androgyne is primarily male, with the addition of a female aspect for the purpose of reproduction. As such, the androgyne is deemed necessary for the ordinary maintenance of society, but without special value. The androgyne makes possible the daily reproduction of the society which claims as its truth, or fiction: "It is only males who are created directly by the gods; those who live righteously return to their star, while those who fail become women."[26] The "heavenly" Aphrodite, the mother of Eros, is not an androgyne. Her attributes are entirely male and she has no mother. The "common and vulgar" Aphrodite, she who looks after reproduction and heterosexuality, is the androgyne.[27]

The truth instituted by the society of male bonding secures its hierarchy and guarantees its continuation through the creation of the powerful and historically enduring lie of "women":

The Primary Lie
Women exist only because men fail to achieve an identity with the ideal.

The Primary Lie Continued
for the Purpose of Reproduction
The best women can hope is to be joined, in subordination, to men.

That domination is not the only form of truth, the only way a culture can sustain its horizons, is decisively suppressed when to the lie of "women" male culture adds the lie of the "androgyne."

II. The Androgyne

Today the prismatic space and time of lesbian touch is covered up, once again, by the androgyne. The androgyne, throughout its history from Plato to the present, has remained within the world established by men's valuation of all that is identical to themselves, by the preeminence of a metaphysic of sight and an ethic of domination.

The androgyne rests on a *logic of agreement*: women, as androgyne, must agree with that truth instituted by the male-defined principles of logic. The truth of the androgyne is not a free and spontaneous discovery but, rather, *truth as correspondence*: women must be in accord with the dictates of male bonding. To women is allotted that range of existence that fulfills, or matches, the expectations of men. Social sanction and obedience to the laws of Aphrodite take precedence over rupture, freedom, and the open.

Women's response is limited to the only naming that can agree with the prescriptions of he who has taken the power to name: naming that conforms to the ways in which male-defined principles of thought conceive women.

The truth of the androgyne is a lie. Through a seeing that attempts to connect the masculine and the feminine, in all their variations, the androgyne remains confined to a surface appearance of life. The androgyne fails to touch the depths of a fourth dimension: the presence of women to women.[28] Moved by the apparent necessity of collecting together the humane qualities of the existing world, the androgyne tears from her skin the living history of a love and friendship that has existed between women, and apart from men. The androgyne may name difference in terms of masculine and feminine, but a still more empowering twofold naming is unsaid. Never named is Rumpelstiltskin: the power of male bonding and the domination of men over women. Unsaid is the experience of lesbian syllables nestled in our bones. Through contact without touch and surfaces without a fourth dimension, the androgyne perpetuates fear of the lesbian.

We fear the lesbian when we tell the lie of the androgyne: when we see ourselves in terms of the *principle of identity*. The identity sought by the androgyne is the possibility to be like a man. The identification of women with "their" men grounds the androgyne's claim to unite the feminine with the masculine:

99

This identification has several sources: on the one hand, identification with her 'personal' oppressor, who is taken as her model...and, on the other hand, *false consciousness*.... [Such identification] bears its own self-contradiction, its own nullification, for identification is the preemptory proof of her non-identity.[29]

The androgyne endeavors to escape her concrete situation by reaching into the stilled sky of the Platonic ideal: a world of apparently neutral ideas. Yet, even the androgyne's claim to promote "a spirit of reconciliation between the sexes,"[30] or to offer a reasonable and unbiased solution in which "the masculine and feminine energies...are combined, but not confused,"[31] bespeaks a neutrality that is always identified with the masculine. As Simone de Beauvoir writes, "man represents both the positive and the neutral, as is indicated by the common use of 'man' to designate human beings."[32]

The androgyne's claim to neutrality is, for women, a claim to non-existence. The promise to neutrality, an artificial "homogenization"[33] of the masculine and the feminine, reduces the reality of women's lives to a fiction. The androgyne becomes what she is not: the skeleton of an ideal identity that can never be her own, the negation of herself and other women.

We forget the lesbian when we tell the lie of the androgyne: when we name ourselves according to *the male-defined principle of difference.* The androgyne is ahistorical. It demands that we dismiss the history of women's naming of ourselves and that we accept a superficial history of men's naming of women as different.

Instead of radically overturning men's naming of women as "the other," the androgyne proposes the redistribution of specific gender differences that assume the male-defined otherness of women. The different activities performed by women and men may be deemed the cause of women's current social situation.[34] Feminine attributes such as non-violence and nurturance may be considered the source of world salvation.[35] Gender-crossing, the mixing of "male" and "female" activities, may be proposed to give a new "balance" to an individual's situation.[36]

Yet, it is not differences in themselves that create an obstacle to freedom, but a specific type of difference: difference that is perpetuated by the society of male bonding and its erasure of women's naming of ourselves. Androgynic gender-crossing, whether it views female "otherness" as a defect or an asset, precludes the possibility that women might claim a history of naming apart from the differences that are mixed and mingled in the patriarchal economy of gender exchange.

We forbid the lesbian when we accept the lie of the androgyne. The androgyne, even when thought under the *principle of equality,* fails to challenge the rules of Aphrodite: women are to share with men an equality; women are to be with men, to manifest with men a sameness of thought and action.

The androgyne's goal, the equality of women and men, disguises the male supremacy of all forms of heterosexual complementarity. In a society in which masculine is "more" and feminine "less," the union of women with men cannot be free of coercion. The androgynic ideal of equality, even as affirmed by Simone de Beauvoir, leaves the female glued perpetually to the male in a necessarily heterosexual union: "the 'female' qualities originate in our oppression but they should be retained after our liberation and men should acquire them. But one must not go too far in the opposite direction."[37] That is, one must not go too far by affirming the freely chosen qualities of a world created by women.

The androgynic assertion, "if there is equality between two persons, there is no longer oppressor and oppressed."[38] fails to conceive of a world where, for women, heterosexuality does not govern all forms of thought and relation. Our embodiment a concept, our touch a matter of equal rights, our deepest existence is set aside. Forbidden is the creative vision of a free and open world of female friends, a vision that might overturn completely the society of male bonding.

▽   ▽   ▽

The androgyne fails in the naming of difference, for it cannot name women apart from men: women as lesbian.

The society of male bonding may peer at the lesbian from afar, but the possibility of the friends' existence defies and defiles its principles of logic. The male-defined principle of identity and its correlates, the principle of difference and the principle of equality, cannot think the lesbian. The coincidence of the friends' touch and tongue is forbidden, but never named, by the fundamental principles of male thought. The male-defined truth as correspondence would obliterate the history of truth. Truth as correctness, as agreement, would deny *truth as the open*.

▽   ▽   ▽

The logic of agreement establishes itself as a major social institution in Western history when the lesbian, seen from the standpoint of Greek male bonding, appears without social sanction.[39] Rejected by the Greek male homosexual poet as a "deserter" and "fugitive," as she who has left behind the "laws of Aphrodite," and referred to only once in Attic literature, the lesbian is made unmentionable, untouchable, taboo, as were both menstruation and the plague of 430 B.C."[40]

Yet, truth as free movement in the open is not new, nor is the lesbian. Attic lesbian love and friendship show "a marked degree of mutual eros" and the obliteration of the usual distinction between a dominant and subordinate partner.[41] Lesbian love and friendship, at least as early as the time of Socrates, break with the male-defined norms of truth.

103

Surviving as an undercurrent in the world of the androgyne is Artemis, "a great spring" and "the source of all the waters." Friends recollect our survival of the Socratic ideal of male bonding and its offspring, the androgyne. We remember ourselves from out of our still living history.

III. The Aqueous

> *Visions may be of images of past, present, or future events. Visions of the past enable us to reassemble the fragments of our history that were distorted by most of the texts before the Glorious age....Present visions serve as communication between companion lovers. ...Future visions are often incomprehensible, but always joyful.*
>
> Wittig & Zeig[42]

Visions trace a tradition of domination, the Socratic ideal of male bonding with its continuation in the androgyne, and a tradition of survival: the song of the Sapphic lyre and the living presence of female friendship. *The tradition of women's survival, in fundamental rupture with a history of domination, is named by its apartness from the world of men.* Apart, but not on the edge, not a fringe element.

Apart, rather, as a living depth that is outside a world of surface appearance. Female friendship, be it experienced as aquatic or otherwise, moves independently of the framework of patriarchal truth. Our historicality is made by the ways in which we build and maintain worlds of meaning that function apart from the stipulations of male bonding. We retrieve our history insofar as we elude the claims of patriarchal truth, insofar as we are oblivious to the demands of mere correctness and obligation. Female friendship emerges, in myriad forms, as we endure through time, freely flowing, tracing out a course. In gentle intimacy, we reach out in trust. Floating and sipping in the springs of the aqueous, we celebrate naming the world of our friendship.

Once, at the origins of philosophy, it was said that water is the source of all. The world was thought to have grown from liquid.[43] In Lesbos, near the deepest of origins, breath and water, *pneuma* and moisture, were conjoined in the sensuous world of women's touch. Artemis, goddess of the springs, was without bounds. The aqueous world floated on her breast.

Yet, all too quickly, the rock upon which philosophy was built, the philosopher's stone, appeared as an androgyne. The philosopher's stone that laid the foundations for male logocentrism was shaped as the union of a hot, masculine, solar part, which could destroy anything, and a feminine lunar part which, through its extreme coldness, could mitigate, but not stop, male destruction.[44] During that time, the springs stopped flowing—except as currents far underground. From then on, the world of water was understood as moist seed, Aristotle's interpretation of Thales' original saying,[45] as *logoi spermatikoi,* or seminal fluid, the Stoic's account of world generation.[46] Virtue resided in semen; *sperma* became identical with "soul."[47] Virtue : soul : semen —the fundamental equation by which philosophy has been constructed starting with the domination of women.[48]

In the coincidence of touch and tongue, friends dissolve the androgyne. Water becomes again the source of all. Floating and gliding on Artemis's breast, friends slip into the aqueous.

NOTES

REMEMBERING:
A TIME I WILL BE MY OWN BEGINNING

[1]H. W. Parke, *A History of the Delphic Oracle* (Oxford: Blackwell, 1939), pp. 4, 17; H. W. Parke, *Greek Oracles* (London: Hutchinson, 1967), pp. 14, 35, 36.

[2]E. R. Dodds, *The Greeks and the Irrational* (Berkeley: University of California Press, 1966), pp. 70, 71, 73.

[3]Plato, *Theaetetus,* 193c. *Collected Dialogues,* eds. Edith Hamilton and Huntington Cairns, trans. F. M. Cornford (New Jersey: Princeton University Press, 1969). Plato's account of memory in the *Theaetetus* is one of the classical discussions of memory in Western philosophy.

[4]Ibid., 194c–195a.

[5]Ibid., 197e.

[6]Adrienne Rich, "Natural Resources," *Dream of a Common Language* (Norton: New York, 1978), p. 65.

[7]Joanna Russ, "The New Misandry," *Amazon Expedition,* eds. Brikby, Harris, Johnson, Newton, O'Wyatt (California: Times Change Press, 1973), p. 27.

[8]Elizabeth Pagedale, "Women Hating Film Elicits Strong Protest," *The Reader* (Chicago, March 13, 1980), p. 10. See also Ntozake Shange, "with no immediate cause," *nappy edges* (New York: St. Martin's Press, 1972), pp. 114–117.

[9]Robin Morgan, *Monster* (New York: Vintage, 1972), p. 83.

[10]Thomas Aquinas, *Summa Theologica,* trans. Fathers of the English Dominican Province (New York: Benziger Brothers, 1947), pp. 714–717, 1341–1344.

[11]Ernest Klein, *A Comprehensive Etymological Dictionary of the English Language* (Amsterdam: Elsevier, 1966), pp. 13, 530, 707; Liddell and Scott, *Greek-English Lexicon* (Oxford: Calrendon, 1925), p. 946; *Oxford English Dictionary* (New York: Oxford University Press, 1972), p. 1263; Eric Partridge, *Origins: A Short Etymological Dictionary of Modern*

English, 4th ed. (London: Routledge & Kegan Paul, 1966), pp. 2, 280; *Webster's New Collegiate* (Massachusetts: Merriam Co., 1973), p. 525.

[12]Pamela Kearon, "Man Hating," *Radical Feminism,* eds. Koedt, Levine, Rapone (New York: Quadrangle, 1973), pp. 79–80.

[13] "Mnemosyne" claims as its roots *memor,* "mindful," and the Greek memēra, "care."

[14]Kathie Sarachild, "The Power of History," *The Feminist Revolution,* ed. Redstockings (New York: Random House, 1978), p. 27.

[15]Monique Wittig, "Paradigm," *Homosexualities and French Literature,* eds. George Strambolian and Elaine Marks (Ithaca: Cornell University Press, 1979), p. 120.

[16]Wittig, *les Guérillères,* trans. David le Vay (New York: Avon, 1973), p. 89.

[17]H. D., "The Flowering of the Rod," *Trilogy* (New York: New Directions Books, 1973), p. 156.

LOOKING AT OUR BLOOD:
A LESBIAN RESPONSE TO
MEN'S TERRORIZATION OF WOMEN

[1]Susan Brownmiller, *Against Our Will: Men, Women and Rape* (New York: Simon and Schuster, 1975), p. 6.

[2] "Seduction, not Assault," from Trinidad, Colorado, *Off Our Backs* (February, 1978), p. 6.

[3]Ann Jones, *Women Who Kill* (New York: Holt, Rinehart and Winston, 1980), p. 287; Andrea Dworkin, *Our Blood* (New York: Harper & Row, 1976), p. 31.

[4]Barbara Mehrhof and Pamela Kearon, "Rape: An Act of Terror," *Radical Feminism,* ed. Koedt, Levine, Rapone, (New York: Quadrangle, 1973), pp. 229, 230.

[5]Martha Shelley, "Terror," *Sisterhood is Powerful,* ed. Robin Morgan (New York: Vintage, 1970), p. 567.

[6]Helen Diner, *Mothers and Amazons* (New York: Doubleday, 1973), pp. 95–105.

[7]The function of the society of Mothers is addressed in Monique Wittig

and Sande Zeig, *Lesbian Peoples: Material for a Dictionary* (New York: Avon, 1979), p. 35.

[8]Laura Clay, "Can Women be fighters?" *Voices from Women's Liberation,* ed. Leslie B. Tanner (New York: New American Library, 1970), p. 90.

[9]Faye Levine, "The Truth About the British Suffragettes," Redstockings, *Feminist Revolution* (New York: Random House, 1978), pp. 46-53.

[10]Elizabeth Robins, "Woman's War: A defense of Militant Suffrage," *McClure's Magazine* (1912), pp. 42-49. I would like to thank Julie Murphy for bringing this article to my attention.

[11]Ida H. Harper, *The Life of Susan B. Anthony* (Indianapolis: Hollenbeck Press, 1898), vol. 2, p. 918.

[12]Levine, "The Truth About the British Suffragettes," p. 33.

[13]Shulamith Firestone, "The Women's Rights Movement in the United States: A New View," New York Radical Women, *Notes from the First Year* (June, 1968), p. 5.

[14]Barbara Deming, as interviewed by Peggy Kornegger in "Cosmic Anarchism: Lesbians in the Sky with Diamonds," *Sinister Wisdom,* no. 12 (1980), p. 8.

[15]Louise Thompson, "Devlin: Even 'Peace' can be a Fighting Word," *Majority Report* (December 11-20, 1976).

[16]Tacie Dejanikus and Stella Dawson, "Women's Pentagon Action," *Off Our Backs* (Janaury, 1981), p. 4.

[17]Pamela McAllister, from her proposal for *Reweaving the Web of Life: Feminism and Nonviolence* (Philadelphia: New Society Publishers, 1982).

[18]Deming, as interviewed by Peggy Kornegger in "Cosmic Anarchism," *op. cit.,* p. 5.

[19]Ibid., p. 6.

[20]Wittig and Zeig, *Lesbian Peoples,* p. 5. See also the original version, Wittig and Zeig, *Brouillon pour un dictionnaire des amantes* (Paris: Grasset, 1976), p. 93.

[21]Ti-Grace Atkinson, *Amazon Odyssey* (New York: Links books, 1974), p. 203.

[22]Monique Wittig, "Entretien avec Monique Wittig," interview by Larence Louppe in *L'art vivant,* vol. 45 (December 73-January 74), pp. 24-25.

[23]Hélène Vivieene Wenzel, *l'opoponax: I still live in here* (unpublished Ph.D. dissertation, University of California at Santa Cruz, 1977), p. 275.

[24]WITCH, "The Witch Manifesto," *Masculine/Feminine,* ed. Betty Roszak and Theodore Roszak (New York: Harper & Row, 1969), p. 257.

[25]Mary Daly, *Gyn/Ecology: The Metaethics of Radical Feminism* (Boston: Beacon Press, 1978), p. 31.

[26]Herbert Marcuse, *Five Lectures* (Boston: Beacon Press, 1970), p. 90.

[27]Simone de Beauvoir, *The Second Sex,* trans. H. M. Parshley (New York: Vintage, 1952), pp. 369-370.

[28]Editors of *questions* féministes, "Variations on Some Common Themes," *Feminist Issues,* vol. 1, no. 1 (1980), p. 13.

[29]Wittig, *les Guérillères,* trans. David LeVay (New York: Avon, 1973), pp. 116, 118.

[30]Valerie Solanas, *SCUM Manifesto* (New York: Solanas, 1977), p. 4.

[31]Susan Elizabeth Cavin, "An hysterical and cross-cultural analysis of sex ratios, female sexuality, and homo-sexual vs. hetero-sexual civilization patterns in relation to the liberation of women" (unpublished dissertation, Rutgers University, 1978), p. 100.

[32]Ibid., p. 275.

[33]Wittig and Zeig, *Lesbian Peoples,* p. 166.

[34]Nor Hall, *Mothers and Daughers,* as cited in Susan Griffin, *Woman and Nature* (New York: Harper & Row, 1978), p. 167.

[35]Olga Broumas, "Imogene Knode," *Heresies,* issue 6, p. 116.

[36]Wittig, *les Guérillères,* p. 143.

[37]Kathleen Barry, "Beyond Pornography: From Defensive Politics to Creating a Vision," *Take Back the Night: Women on Pornography,* ed. Laura Lederer (New York: Morrow, 1980), p. 312.

[38]Marcia Womongold, *Pornography: License to Kill* (Massachusetts: New England Press, 1979), p. 14.

[39]Radical Lesbians, "The Woman Identified Woman," *Radical Feminism,* ed. Koedt, Levine, Rapone, p. 240.

[40]Judy Grahn, "She Who," *The Work of a Common Woman* (California: Diana Press, 1978), p. 87.

[41]Wittig, *les Guérillères,* p. 93.

MOTHERHOOD:

THE ANNIHILATION OF WOMEN

[1]I would like to thank Julie Murphy for suggesting the phrase, "a philosophy of evacuation."

[2]Simone de Beauvoir, *The Second Sex,* trans. H. M. Parshley (New York: Vintage, 1974), p. 72.

[3]de Beauvoir, "Talking to de Beauvoir," *Spare Rib* (March, 1977), p. 2.

[4]Shulamith Firestone, *The Dialectic of Sex* (New York: Bantam, 1971), p. 72.

[5]Ti-Grace Atkinson, *Amazon Odyssey* (New York: Links Books, 1974), p. 1.

[6]Monique Wittig and Sande Zeig, *Brouillon pour un dictionnaire des amantes* (Paris: Grasset, 1976), p. 94; Wittig, "One is not born a Woman," *Feminist Issues,* vol. 1, no. 2 (Winter, 1981), p. 1.

[7]de Beauvoir, "Talking to de Beauvoir," p. 2.

[8]Atkinson, "Interview with Ti-Grace Atkinson," *Off Our Backs,* vol. 9, no. 11 (December, 1973), p. 3.

[9]Andrea Dworkin, *Pornography: Men Possessing Women* (New York: Perigree, 1981), p. 222.

[10]Wittig, "Paradigm," *Homosexualities and French Literature,* eds. George Stambolian and Elaine Marks (Ithaca: Cornell University Press, 1979), pp. 118, 119.

[11]*WIN News,* vol. 7, no. 4 (1981), p. 68. Citation from the Soviet Women's Committee, "Soviet Women's Committee" booklet.

[12]A more "sophisticated" appeal to science is misleading for similar reasons. Feminist biologists are currently questioning accounts of egg and sperm production, for instance, in an attempt to dislodge sexist assumptions with respect to their production and union.

[13]*WIN News,* vol. 6, no. 2 (1980), p. 76. U.S. Department of Labor, "Facts About Women Heads of Households and Heads of Families."

[14]Catharine MacKinnon, *Sexual Harrassment of Working Women* (New Haven: Yale University Press, 1979), p. 221.

[15]Iion Wieder, "Accouche!" *questions féministes* no. 5 (February, 1979), pp. 53–72.

[16]*The Oxford English Dictionary* (Oxford: Clarendon Press, 1933), p. 236.

Notes

¹⁷ de Beauvoir, *The Second Sex,* p. 72.

¹⁸Ranya Rapp, "Women, Religion and Archaic Civilizations: An Introduction" *Feminist Studies,* vol. 4, no. 3 (October, 1978), p. 1.

¹⁹Anne Barstow, "The Neolithic Goddess at Çatal Hüyük," *Feminist Studies,* vol. 4, no. 3 (October, 1978), p. 12.

²⁰James Mellart, *The Archaeology of Ancient Turkey* (London: Bodley Head, 1978), p. 20; E. O. James, *The Cult of the Mother Goddess* (London: Thames & Hudson, 1958), pp. 22.

²¹James, *The Cult of the Mother Goddess,* p. 23.

²²Mellart, *The Neolithic Near East* (London: Thames & Hudson, 1975), p. 99.

²³Ibid., p. 107.

²⁴Ibid., p. 167.

²⁵James, *op. cit.,* pp. 17, 18.

²⁶Mellart, *Çatal Hüyük* (New York: McGraw Hill 1967), p. 183; Mellart, *The Archaeology of Ancient Turkey,* p. 20.

²⁷Ibid, p. 142.

²⁸Mellart, *Çatal Hüyük,* p. 181.

²⁹Catherine Deudon, "Le Colonialism hétéro," *Actuel,* no. 38 (1974), p. 15.

³⁰Martin Heidegger, "The Age of the World Picture,"*The Question of Technology,* trans. William Lovitt (New York: Harper & Row, 1977), pp. 129-130.

³¹Ibid., p. 135.

³²Ibid., p. 134.

³³Ibid., p. 135.

³⁴Dworkin, *Pornography,* pp. 108, 109.

³⁵Jane Harrison, *Prolegomena to the Study of Greek Religion,* 3rd ed. (Cambridge: Cambridge University Press, 1922), pp. 302, 303.

³⁶de Beauvoir, *The Second Sex,* p. 155.

³⁷Colette Guillaumin, "Race et Nature: Système des marques. Idée de groupe naturel et rapports sociaux," *Pluriel,* no. 11 (1977), pp. 39-55. Guillaumin develops the concept of the mark to analyze racial oppression.

³⁸Ibid., pp. 48, 54, 55.

³⁹Ibid., p. 49.

⁴⁰Ibid., p. 45.

⁴¹Ibid., p. 55.

⁴²Fran Hosken, "The Case Histories: The Western World," *The Hosken Report,* 2d rev. ed. (Lexington Massachusetts, 1979), p. 11.

⁴³Ibid., "Medical Facts and Summary," p. 2.

⁴⁴Ibid., "Case Histories," p. 9.

⁴⁵Ibid., "The Reasons Given," p. 5.

⁴⁶Ibid., p. 6.

⁴⁷*WIN News,* vol. 7, no. 2 (1981), p. 39. Citation from *The New National Black Monitor,* (October, 1980).

⁴⁸Hosken, "Forward," *The Hosken Report,* p. 3.

⁴⁹Ibid.

⁵⁰*WIN News,* vol. 6, no. 2 (1980), p. 30. From Edna Adan Ismail, *Genital Operations: Their Physical and Mental Effects and Complications*

⁵¹Hosken, "Medical Facts and Summary," *The Hosken Report,* p. 6.

⁵²*WIN News,* vol. 6, no. 4 (1980), p. 45. From the New South Whales Humanist Society, "Report on Genital Mutilation from Australia."

⁵³Hosken, "The Reasons Given," *The Hosken Report,* p. 4.

⁵⁴*WIN News,* vol. 7, no. 4 (1981), p. 34. Report by Dr. Abu Hassan Abu in "Workshop on Eradicating Female Circumcision in the Sudan."

⁵⁵*Win News,* vol. 7, no. 2 (1981). From *Journal-American* (January 3, 1981).

⁵⁶*International Tribunal on Crimes Against Women,* eds. Diana Russell and Nicole Van de Ven (California: Les Femmes, 1976), pp. 31–33.

⁵⁷*WIN News,* vol. 7, no. 3 (1981), p. 22. From AGENOR, "Abortion: The Facts/ European Survey."

⁵⁸*WIN News,* vol. 7, no. 4 (1981), p. 17. From World Health Organization, "Towards a Better Future: Maternal and Child Health."

⁵⁹*WIN News,* vol. 6, no. 4 (1980), p. 37. From "Population Reports" (Series F/ Number 7/ July 1980).

⁶⁰*WIN News,* vol. 7, no. 3 (1981), p. 22. From AGENOR, "Abortion: The Facts/ European Survey."

⁶¹Wieder, *op. cit.,* p. 69.

⁶²*WIN News,* vol. 7, no. 4 (1981), p. 24. From The Population Institute, *International Dateline.*

⁶³*WIN News,* vol. 7, no. 3 (1981), p. 16. From World Health Organization, "Sixth Report on the World Health Situation."

⁶⁴Ibid.

⁶⁵Ibid.

⁶⁶Jalna Hammer, "Sex Predetermination, Artificial Insemination and the Maintenance of Male-Dominated Culture, *Women, health, and reproduction,* ed. Helen Roberts (London: Routledge & Kegan Paul, 1981), pp. 167, 168.

[67]Ibid., p. 176.

[68]Jalna Hammer and Pat Allen, "La Science de la reproduction—solution finale?" *questions féministes,* vol. 5 (February, 1979), p. 39.

[69]Elizabeth Fisher, *Woman's Creation* (New York: Doubleday, 1980), p. 335.

[70]Wittig and Zeig, *Lesbian Peoples: Material for a Dictionary* (New York: Avon, 1979), p. 83.

[71]Hammar and Allen, *op. cit.,* p. 39.

[72]Wittig and Zeig, *op. cit.,* p. 76.

[73]Ibid., p. 75.

[74]*WIN News,* vol. 7, no. 4 (1981), p. 19. *The American Journal of Obstetrics and Gynecology* (July, 1981), shows that the mortality rate in the United States for infants aided by midwife-assisted deliveries is nine per thousand births, in comparison with nearly seventeen per thousand births among physician-aided deliveries. Such alternative means have positive implications for women as mothers.

[75]Julie Murphy, personal communication, December, 1981.

[76]*WIN News,* vol. 7, no. 4 (1981), pp. 23, 24. From The Population Institute, *International Dateline.* See Jeffner Allen, "Women and Food: Feeding Ourselves," *The Journal of Social Philosophy,* 1984, pp. 34–41.

[77]*WIN News,* vol. 7, no. 4 (1981), p. 73. From the National Commission on Working Mothers, "Women at Work: News about the 80%."

[78]Hosken, "Editorial," *WIN News,* vol. 7, no. 2 (1981), p. 1.

[79]*WIN News,* vol. 7, no. 1 (1981), p. 21. From World Bank Headquarters, "Education: A World Bank Sector Policy Paper."

[80]Hosken, "Editorial," *WIN News,* vol. 6, no. 3 (1980), p. 1.

[81]*WIN News,* vol. 7, no. 4 (1981), p. 6. From U.N. Conference on New and Renewable Sources of Energy, "Conference Report."

THE NAMING OF DIFFERENCE: TRUTH AND FEMALE FRIENDSHIP

[1]Sappho, *Sappho,* trans. Mary Barnard (Berkeley: University of California Press, 1958), p. 8.

²Robert Graves, *Les Mythes grecs,* trans. Mounir Hafez (Paris: Librarie Fayard, 1968), pp. 632, 75.

³Maliña Poquez, "La rupture épistémologique fondamentale," *questions féministes* IV (1978), pp. 3-12.

⁴Monique Wittig, *The Lesbian Body,* trans. David LeVay (New York: Avon, 1973), p. 14. See also Mary Carruthers, "The Re-vision of the Muse: Adrienne Rich, Audre Lorde, Judy Grahn, Olga Broumas," *The Hudson Review* (Summer, 1983), p. 309.

⁵Nicholas of Cusa, cited by Joan Stambaugh in her "Introduction," Heidegger, *Identity and Difference,* trans. Stambaugh (New York: Harper & Row: 1969), p. 9. See Heidegger's critique of the logocentric principles of thought of Western philosophy and his analysis of the history of truth.

⁶Hélène Cixous, "Sorties," *New French Feminisms,* eds. Elaine Marks and Isabelle de Courtivron (Amherst: University of Massachusetts, 1980), pp. 92, 93.

⁷Olga Broumas, *Caritas* (Eugene: Jackrabbit Press, 1976), p. 5.

⁸Maurice Merleau-Ponty, *The Phenomenology of Perception,* trans. Colin Smith (New York: Routledge and Kegan Paul, 1962), pp. 235-237.

⁹J. Grimm, "Rumpelstiltskin," *Household Stories from the Collection of the Brothers Grimm,* trans. Lucy Crane (New York: Dover, 1963), p. 231.

¹⁰Broumas, *op. cit.,* p. 3. See also Broumas, "Rumpelstiltskin," *Beginning with O* (New Haven: Yale University Press, 1977), p. 65.

¹¹Martha Courtot, *Journey* (Tucson: Up Press, 1977), p. 8.

¹²K. J. Dover, *Greek Homosexuality* (New York: Vintage, 1980), p. 154.

¹³Horst Hutter, *Politics as Friendship* (Waterloo: Wilfred Laurier University Press, 1978), p. 16.

¹⁴Dover, *op. cit.,* p. 164. See also Plato, *Phaedrus* 250d.

¹⁵Plato, *Republic* 508d, trans. Alan Bloom (Basic Books: New York, 1968).

¹⁶Ibid.

¹⁷Dover, *op. cit.,* p. 84.

¹⁸Ibid., p. 156; Hutter, *op. cit.,* pp. 66, 77.

¹⁹Plato, *Laws* 781b trans. A. E. Taylor, *Collected Dialogues,* eds. Edith Hamilton and Huntington Cairns (New Jersey: Princeton University Press, 1969).

²⁰Hermann Bengston, *The Greeks and the Persians* (London: Weidenfeld & Nicolson, 1968), pp. 149-150.

Notes

[21]Ibid., p. 150. See also Plato, *Republic* 514a, 515b.

[22]Bengston, *op. cit.,* pp. 149, 150.

[23]Dover, *op. cit.,* pp. 162, 164.

[24]Ibid., p. 101.

[25]Ibid.

[26]Anne Dickason, "Anatomy and Destiny: The Role of Biology in Plato's Views of Women," *Women and Philosophy: Toward a Theory of Liberation,* eds. Carol Gould and Marx Wartofsky (New York: Putnam, 1976), pp. 46, 48. See also Plato, *Timaeus* 91a and *Symposium* 191-192.

[27]Plato, *Symposium* 181b, c.

[28]For other critiques of the androgyne see Mary Daly, *Beyond God the Father* (Boston: Beacon Press, 1973), p. xi; Adrienne Rich, "Natural Resources," *Dream of a Common Language* (New York: Norton, 1978), p. 66; and Janice Raymond, *The Transsexual Empire: The Making of the She-Male* (Boston: Beacon Press, 1979), p. 159.

[29]C.D., "Nos amis et nous: La Haine de soi comme fondement du 'gauchisme' féminine," *questions féministes,* I (1978), p. 43. Translated by Jeffner Allen.

[30]Carolyn Heilbrun, *Toward a Recognition of Androgyny* (New York: Harper & Row, 1973), p. x.

[31]June Singer, *Androgyny: Toward a New Theory of Sexuality* (New York: Anchor Books, 1977), p. 326.

[32]Simone de Beauvoir, *The Second Sex,* trans. H. M. Parshley (New York: Vintage, 1974), p. xviii.

[33]Mary Anne Warren, *The Nature of Woman* (California: Edge Press, 1980), p. 27.

[34]Anne Ferguson, "Androgyny as an Ideal of Human Development," *Feminism and Philosophy,* eds. Vetterling-Braggin, Elliston, English, p. 61.

[35]Herbert Marcuse, "Marxism and Feminism," *Women's Studies* II (1974), pp. 286, 287.

[36]Heilbrun, *op. cit.,* p. x.

[37]Beauvoir, "Talking to Simone de Beauvoir," *Spare Rib* (1972), pp. 7-9.

[38]This assertion is analyzed by Monique Wittig, "La pensée straight," *questions* féministes, VII (1980), p. 50.

[39]Hutter, *op. cit.*

[40]Dover, *op. cit,* p. 172.

[41]Ibid., p. 177.

[42]Monique Wittig and Sande Zeig, *Lesbian Peoples: Material for a Dictionary,* (New York: Avon, 1979), p. 160.

[43]The idea that philosophy must return to water was suggested to me by Julie Murphy. See Reginald Allen, "Introduction," *Greek Philosophy: Thales to Aristotle,* ed. Reginald Allen (New York: The Free Press, 1966), pp. 1, 2.

[44]Raymond, "Transsexualism: An Etiological and Ethical Analysis," p. 436.

[45]Aristotle, *Metaphysics* 983b 6, *Greek Philosophy: Thales to Aristotle,* ed. Allen, p. 30.

[46]Proclus, "SUF II, 717," *Greek and Roman Philosophy After Aristotle,* ed. J. L. Saunders (New York: Free Press, 1966), p. 96.

[47]Hutter, *op. cit.,* p. 79; Dickason, *op. cit.,* pp. 51, 52.

[48]Cixous, *op. cit.,* p. 92.